# Guided Meditations for Self-Healing

*Beginners Meditation to Heal Your Body.
Mindfulness Therapy Including
Breathing, Vipassana Script, Chakra
Healing, Yoga Sutras, Techniques for
Deep Sleep & More*

D1557194

# Table of Content

# Introduction

Congratulations on purchasing *Guided Meditations for Self-Healing*: *Beginners Meditation to Heal Your Body. Mindfulness Meditation Including Breathing, Vipassana Script, Chakra Healing, Yoga Sutras, Meditation for Deep Sleep, And More*, and thank you for doing so. The world is full of problems, and everyone has something to worry about. With a busy schedule and the hard economy, the problems people face get too complex by the day, and our inability to deal with the challenges cause a great deal of stress and anxiety. However, adopting meditation techniques that can help in overcoming stress is critical, which is why the information you find in this book is very important it can help you transform your life for the better.

To that end, the following chapters will discuss the key meditation techniques necessary to enhance the health of your body and soul and reduce any stressful events in your life. This means that you will have to review your inner thoughts on every situation that affects your life, how to solve the situation using alternative meditation solutions, and the various chakra tactics that would help to improve your wellbeing. With stress out of your way, you will then learn how to keep your energy and spirit high and the ways to cultivate a mental attitude that will bring peace and happiness. Learning these meditation tips to increase your energy and keep yourself motivated will help you to remain calm in every situation, that may otherwise cause you stress. Finally, you will get to learn ways to improve your willpower through the use of meditation and breathing techniques.

There are several books on the subject of meditation in the market, thanks again for considering this one! I hope you enjoy reading!

# Chapter 1: Introduction to Meditation

*"MEDITATION can help us embrace our worries, our fear, our anger, and that is very HEALING. We let our own natural capacity of healing do the work."— Thich Nhat Hanh*

One time, Buddha was asked, "What have you achieved from meditation?" "Nothing," he said, "But let me tell you what I have lost: anxiety, anger, insecurity, depression, and fear of death." He also told a traveler who wanted to know who he was, "I am awake." In his three words defining himself, *I am awake*; Buddha was able to deliver the whole teachings of Buddhism. The term "Buddha" means 'to be awake' to the surrounding, including life and death.

That is what meditation does: it makes an individual awake. The practice of meditation does not mean that one should become a spiritual being or a Buddhist. It enables one to fulfill one's own capacity to be awakened. It enables one to become more present, more mindful, more awake, and more compassionate. In fact, to be awake through meditation means discovering open-hearted, natural, and non-judgmental awareness of the body, our thoughts, and feelings. We can bring this kind of awareness to understand what is going through our minds.

But what is meditation?

## Definition of Meditation

Meditation refers to the approach used to train the mind, similar to a fitness program that is used to train the body. It is an ancient practice, which helps us to control our own minds, and ultimately our lives in order to discover ourselves.

You could say that meditation is a way of recharging your own batteries and a means to calm down your mind. In many instances, our minds are taken over, which hinders us from having stable thoughts. Through meditation, we are able to feel and control our thoughts without losing sleep of using so much energy. It is through meditation that we can control our thoughts and minds, and turn off our minds from what we do not need to feel or think about anymore.

Meditation is a strategy that is key to living and feeling well to achieve a happy life. It helps in the elimination of worries, bad thoughts, anxiety, and any other factors that may hinder us from being happy. If carried out on a regular basis, meditation helps in the mitigation of anxiety and stress.

## Benefits of Meditation

When talk about mindfulness pops up, a lot of humans will still try to think that meditation is the sphere of free spirits who have fun out on woven grass mat somewhere. There is the fact that you should know, and the truth is, there is nothing woo-woo in connection with mindfulness and consciousness meditation. These life occurrences have always been there ever since, and nearly every divine path assimilates approximately form of them. There are interesting facts that you should know about meditation, as discussed below.

1. **Meditation will make you feel happy**

   A lot of people who usually meditate will all the time have a happy life, unlike those who don't. meditation generally has been able to increase the flow of productive thoughts and positive feelings. When you take a few moments meditating most of the time, it can make some huge difference in your life. It has been proven scientifically that meditation brings happiness. A study was done to a group of Buddhist monks when they were meditating to prove this claim. The pre-frontal cortex of the monk's mind was seen to be more active.

2. **Meditation will assist you to control nervousness, despair, and strain**

   The enhancement potential of meditation should never be underestimated. A study that has been conducted at the University of Wisconsin showed that meditation would bring psychological effects to mind. For instance, the researchers found out that the mind controls stress and anxiety shrink when meditation is practiced constantly.

When you focus on the moment by moment knowledge, meditators are trying to teach the brain to be calm, even when going through stressful moments. Due to this, you will also experience knowingly reduced anxiety because of not being sure of what will come along in the future.

## 3. You shouldn't be a religious leader for you to meditate

Mind work meditation app organizers have a belief that meditation is probably there to benefit anyone without being bias. Meditation is beyond doctrine, and it is about creating calmness, learning how to be aware, and decluttering the brain. Contemplation has been a vital component in most of the world religions. You are not supposed to be a religious person for you to meditate. Such news is the best for one in five Americans who see themselves as spiritual but not religious. Pew Research Centre in January published their findings that told us how the mainstream mindfulness meditation had been recognized in the US despite religious connection.

## 4. Benefits of meditation are immediate

A lot of several health impacts that come about due to meditation are the reasons why so many people opt or think of trying the meditation practice. Some of their benefits can begin making their effects felt fast immediately you begin sitting. The sense of being calm, and having a peace of mind are the communal experiences, despite the feeling being fleet and elusive. There is an article that was published in Forbes online, and attorney Jeena Cho listed six scientific benefits that had been proven and that you should expect, including a decrease in unspoken race and age prejudice. Other people also argue that meditation is making them have opposite effects, and this is because their minds are getting busier than ever. You are advised to stick with it and try to make your sessions to be short. Meditation is not all about wiping the slate of your brain clean, but it is about being knowledgeable of what is seen. This will make you step ahead, and you will have noticed how busy your brain can be.

5. **Meditation will make you sleep easily**

Insomnia is a trying, difficult, and troubling disorder. Most of the humans always talk about having sleepless nights. You should note that almost a third of the American population has been suffering due to some form of sleep deficiency, and this can be irregular or long-lasting. You may be among those people who spend their time staring at the ceiling trying to count sheep the whole night, but to no avail, then with such experiences, the best solution is meditation. There is an article in the Harvard Health Blog that authorizes that meditation will trigger a relaxation reply. Due to this, most people will tend to have the opposite problem and will fall to sleep immediately; they start to meditate.

## 6. Meditation will give you a sharp memory

Having assisted you in being happy and improving your wellbeing, meditation will still assist your memory to be sharp, and your concentration will remain to be steady. When you have mindful meditation, you can train in the remaining conscious of the present moment in an easygoing method. Subsequently, interruptions are less and less likely to carry you away. This is a reason why you should try to meditate.

## 7. Meditation will make you generate kindness

Other kinds of meditation will increase positive feelings and actions to yourself and other people. There is a type of mediation called the Metta that is also referred to as loving-kindness meditation. It always starts by improving your kind thoughts and feelings to yourself. When you practice, you will be able to learn about extending kindness and forgiveness to other people. It will be to your friends, acquaintances, and your enemies too. There have been several studies about this kind of meditation demonstrating its capability to have additional peoples' kindness to themselves and other people.

A study done to adults erratically dispensed to a program that had inclusion of love and kindness meditation found that these reimbursements were dose dependent. In short, when many people are putting their effort towards Metta meditation, the more positive feelings they will go through. Another research also shows that the positive feelings that you will build through Metta meditation will enhance social anxiety, decrease marriage violence, and assist in controlling anger. You can't imagine that there are people who still want to be convinced even after going through the meditation facts above.

# Chapter 2: Mindfulness Meditation

*"Meditation gives a clear understanding about body and brain interface with consciousness"- Amir Ray*

It doesn't matter what you are thinking about at the moment. It could be about family, work, school, dinner, and many more, it is quite natural for you to get lost in your thoughts. Sometimes you get so engrossed about your past events or worry about the future expectations so that you end up stressed and anxious.

Mindfulness meditation is a mental training practice that can significantly help you in the situations mentioned above. This kind of meditation helps bring you and your thoughts into the present. It helps you to focus your emotions, thoughts, and the sensations which you are going through "in the now."

Although initially, you may experience some challenges controlling your thoughts, with time and a lot of practice, you will be able to experience the beautiful benefits of mindful meditation, which includes being less stressed and anxious, and reduction of symptoms of mental problems such as the IBS.

The basic concepts behind mindfulness meditation techniques include breathing practice, mental imagery, awareness of your body and mind as well as relaxation involving your muscles and mind.

Mindfulness is your ability to be fully present and being aware of where you are, what you are doing, and being in control of your actions such that you are not overwhelmed with what is going on around you.

While mindfulness is something you naturally possess, you tend to develop and manifest it further when you practice it daily — being mindful means bringing your awareness to what you are directly experiencing through your senses, thoughts, or emotions. Studies show that when you train your brain to be mindful, you succeed in remodeling your mind to wake up the inner workings involving the mental, physical, and emotional processes.

Mindful meditation also requires you to venture into the workings of your minds. You explore your sensations, emotions, and thoughts so that your curiosity about the functioning of your mind is awakened. The good thing about mindful meditation is that it is always readily available to us; all you need to take time to pause and breathe for your awareness to be triggered.

# The Basics of Mindfulness Meditation Practice

Mindfulness meditations help you to put some space between yourself and how you react whenever you are faced with any situation. The following practices will guide you to tune into mindful meditation daily:

a. **Set aside some time** - All you need is to set aside some time from your busy schedule to engage in meditations. Getting off other activities is the most crucial requirement for effective mindful mediation. You won't need any special equipment, like a bench or chair. Just set some time and space, and you are good to go.

b. **Observe your present moment as it is** - The goal of mindfulness is for you to pay close attention to what you are experiencing at the present moment without judging it. It is not about quieting your mind or attempting to achieve some state of long-lasting calm. Focus on the sensations, thoughts, and imaginations of your mind at that present moment.

c. **Let your judgments pass** - In case you notice any thoughts during your practices, you shouldn't suppress them. Instead, take a mental note of them and let them pass.

d. **Return to the present moment** - Once your judgments have passed, focus back your mind to the present, making observations of the current as it is. Mindfulness is about returning your thoughts to the present, sometimes severally during your entire practice. Your mind tends to be carried off easily by the myriads of thoughts crossing it. You must refocus your mind on the present thought.

e. **Don't judge your wandering** - You shouldn't be hard on yourself every time your mind wanders off during the practice. It is common for all humans to have thoughts propping up instinctively, and without any warning, you should, therefore, learn how to recognize when your mind wandered off to gently bring it back and refocus it on the present.

## Important Mindfulness Techniques

We can practice mindfulness in different ways. All of the available methods focus on how you can achieve a state of alertness and relaxation to focus your attention on your thoughts and sensations without judging them. The following are some of the meditation techniques:

**Basic mindfulness technique** - This technique requires you to sit quietly in the same spot and focus on your breathing. You can also focus on saying a single word that you silently say over and over again. You should allow your thoughts to come in and out without judgment, and each time, you return to your focus on the breath.

**Body sensations** - You should also take note of small and subtle body sensations such as an itch or tingling. Don't judge the sensations, instead allow them to pass. You should take note of all feelings taking place in every part of your body from your head to the toe.

**Sensory** - You should also take note of the sensory sensations such as the sights, sounds, smells, touches, or taste. Give them names and let them pass without any judgment.

**Emotions -** You should also let your emotions manifest without suppressing or judging them. You should name your feelings in a steady and relaxed way, such as "joy, anger, happiness."

**Cravings and urges** - You should let your cravings for addictive substances or behaviors to be present. Allow them to pass without judgment. Take a conscious mental note of how your body feels when the specific cravings enter.

# How to Practice Mindfulness Meditation?

Mindfulness meditation focuses on your breathing. It emphasizes the need for you to focus your physical sensation of breathing as an anchor to your present moment. All your thoughts, emotions, sounds will always come back to your next breath whenever it wanders off. Your mind will always come back whenever you breathe from wherever it had wandered off to.

Before you start the meditation, it is always wise to set an amount of time you need to do the practice. In case it is your first time, strive to set aside a short time of let's say five to ten minutes. You can gradually add this time as you gain experience to a maximum of 45 minutes or one hour.

You can also choose whatever time suits your schedule. Many people opt to practice in the morning or in the evening. But there is no specified time; you can do your meditation even during your lunch break, so long as you are comfortable with the practice.

You should then find a suitable spot in your home or office. Such a place must be conducive enough with no distractions. It should also be well lit with enough aeration if the area has sufficient natural light, the better.

The following is an easy meditation guide you can use to practice mindfulness meditation at the comfort of your home:

I. **Sit comfortably** - You need to find a spot that gives you some comfortable sitting. You can choose to spread a mat on the ground and sit on it, but if you find the bare ground uncomfortable, then you can sit on a comfortable plastic chair or a bench.

II. **It is also advisable to wear some comfortable clothing** - So that you don't become distracted by the discomfort of sitting for long hours.

III. **Take note of your legs** - Monitor your legs closely. If you are sitting on a cushion, then you can comfortably cross your legs together in front of you. In case you are sitting on a chair, you should comfortably rest the bottoms of your feet on the floor.

IV. **Straighten your upper body** - You should then straighten your upper body to assume a straight sitting posture. Let your spinal cord assume its natural position. You should, therefore, avoid stiffening it.

V. **Take note of what your arms are doing** - You should place your upper arms in a parallel position to your upper body. You then rest your palms comfortably on your legs. Let your arms naturally rest of the most comfortable part of your legs.

VI. **Soften your gaze** - You should then drop your gin a little to let your gaze focus on the ground, in a downward but gentle fall. This doesn't mean you close your eyes completely. All you need to do is to let your gaze fall on whatever appears om your view without focusing your eyes on it. Then try to get rid of all the thoughts of the past and future and put all focus on the present reflections.

VII. **Focus on your breathing** - Afterward, you should then focus on the physical sensations of your breath. Feel your breathtaking note of the air moving through your nose or mouth, take note of how the rising and falling of your belly and chest as you take in the air and breath it out.

VIII. **Notice whenever the mind wanders off from breathing** - You should expect your attention to leave your breath and wander off to other places. However, this shouldn't bother you; it is quite common for everyone to have their attention wander from their present thoughts. You shouldn't, therefore, try to block them from wandering off from your breath. You shouldn't also eliminate the thoughts once it focusses on other things. Instead, once you notice your mind wandering off from your breath, you should gently return it to your breath. You should also pay a lot of attention to how your breathing changes and the difference it brings to your body.

IX. **Watch every thought** - You then watch every thought that comes and go. It could be thoughts of worry, anxiety, fear, or hope. When these thoughts register in your mind, you should not suppress, ignore, or eliminate them. You should take note of them while you maintain your calmness. You can make use of your breath to anchor them.

X. **You should be kind to yourself when your mind wanders off** - It is normal for your mind to wander off severally in the course of your practice. Instead of preventing them, learn to make a silent observation without reacting to them. All you should do id to sit and to pay a lot of attention. This may be a challenge for you, but again there is nothing you can do to prevent your mind from wandering off your breath. It will eventually come back to your breath once again, make an observation, and patiently wait without judgment or expectations. You should observe where your mind goes to without judging it, then gently return to your breathing.

XI. **Once you are ready, lift your gaze gently-** when you are ready, you can then gently lift your gaze, and in case you had closed your eyes, open them. Let your gaze take in the surrounding. Allow your senses to take note of the surrounding for noises, sounds, smell, color, etc. take note of how your body feels at that moment. Sit for another minute or two as you make yourself to be aware of where you are before you gradually get up.

## How to Incorporate Mindfulness to Your Daily Life?

Mindfulness can be practiced anywhere and at any time of the day. No law limits mindfulness to sitting in a cushion. You can incorporate the essential techniques of mindfulness to your everyday activities and tasks. Such events provide a lot of opportunities for you to carry out your mindfulness practice. You can cultivate mindfulness in your daily routine through some of the following practices:

### While Washing Dishes

When you are busy doing the dishes, you hardly get any distractions from everyone else. The fact that you get little distractions when doing the dishes offers you an excellent opportunity to try some mindfulness. As you clean your dishes and kitchen, you should train your mind to focus on the physical activity, making a note of the warm water on your hand, the sound of the clanking utensils, and the sound of the running water. All these activities and their accompanying sensations will help your mind focus on the present.

## Brushing Your Teeth

You brush your teeth daily, sometimes more than twice each day. This could offer you an excellent opportunity to practice mindfulness meditation. Take note of the brush in your hand, the feet on the ground, and how your arm moves up and down as you undertake your brushing.

## Driving

It is quite easy to let your mind wander off when you are driving. But you should use your mindfulness power to anchor your thoughts to the present, focusing on the inside of your car. You can start by turning off your car radio or putting on some cool, soothing music. Then gently bring back your mind to the present, paying attention to where you are and what you are experiencing.

**Exercising**

You can practice mindfulness while atop your treadmill. Just focus on your breathing and where your feet are in space as you work on your treadmill. Pay close attention to the way you take in and out your breath. Notice how the pattern your legs create as your feet hit the mill or the ground.

## The Benefits of Mindfulness Meditation

Mindfulness meditation can bring a lot of improvements to physical as well as psychological symptoms. It can also bring positive changes in your health, attitudes, and behaviors of the individuals who practice it consistently. The following are some of the important benefits of mindfulness:

## Mindfulness Improves Your General Well Being

If you incorporate mindfulness into your daily routine, then you should expect an improvement in your attitudes to help you live a satisfying life. When you are mindful, it is easier for you to enjoy the pleasures of life as they occur. You also become more engaged in your daily activities. Mindfulness also empowers you to better deal with any adverse occurrence in your life.

When you focus on here and now, you are less likely to be trapped by worries of the future or even the regrets of the past. You are also less preoccupied with your success or self-esteem because you tend to live a happy and content life free from any connections to material things.

## Mindfulness is Key to Your Physical Health

Studies reveal you can use mindfulness to improve your physical health. Mindfulness helps to release such problems as stress, high blood pressure, chronic pain, insomnia, among many other health problems you might be facing.

## Mindfulness Improves Your Mental Health

Studies reveal mindfulness can be used to alleviate various mental health problems that people face. Recent years have seen psychotherapist turning to mindfulness meditation to several issues which include, anxiety disorders, depression, drug abuse, conflict among couples, and obsessive-compulsive disorders.

**Improve Your Attention**

Studies have established that when you practice mindfulness for even a short time, your ability to sustain attention is much improved. Your working memory, the functioning of the mind, and Visio's special processing are also much enhanced with mindfulness.

**Helps You Sleep Better**

Researchers determined that mindfulness much helps adults diagnosed with severe sleep disturbances to improve their sleep quality. It dramatically reduces the sleep-related impairment, which has negative implications on the quality of the life you live.

# Chapter 3: A Breathing Meditation

*"Feelings come and go like clouds in a windy sky. Conscious breathing is my anchor."– Thich Nhat Hahn*

You may be wondering how you can cultivate your mindfulness. The best way that can help you do this is by meditation. The best process is by focusing your attention on the way you are breathing. This kind of practice is also referred to as mindful breathing. When you put some time aside for practicing conscious breathing, then you will have a manageable impact to focus your attention on the way you breathe daily. You should be able to cool down yourself when your tempers flares, and you feel they are sharpening your ability to concentrate.

Meditation is one of the best ways that you can use in relieving anxiety and assist you in gaining your center. So many people have found it very difficult to achieve an evident mind. When you are meditating while breathing, then this will be when you focus on the depth and stride on how you inhale and exhale. When you do this, you will be enhancing your breathing, and this will assist in preventing distraction. When you are aware and prepared for meditating, and you can understand your breathing techniques, this will help you to have peace of mind without limits.

## 1. Formulating your account

### Get a quiet, bland space

You should get a place that has no loud noises or some odors that can easily distract you. Another thing to note, avoid sites that have too much decoration because this can easily divert your attention. Get somewhere that works out the best for you when you are in a peaceful state of mind. You can prefer indoor spaces that have fewer distracting sounds, either way, and you can get a place outside in cases where you want fresh air and make sure you are distant from automotive and people.

## Find a lenient surface

A lot of people always sit down when they are meditating; thus, you are advised to get somewhere that you can be able to sit down with comfort for more time. You can sit on a carpet or soft grass, which is ideal on this occasion. Possibly you can use a yoga mat or at times, a towel.

## Clear our interruptions

You should turn off your phone or put it in silence mode or anything that may distract you with noise. When you have people around you, ask them for some few minutes alone because you plan to have a meditation. You can be having pets like dogs, cats, that may want your attention, put them in some that they can't reach you and disrupt you. Ask the people you are staying with to give you 30 minutes without interruption unless there is an emergency. Tell them you will be meditating, and you have to maintain a lot of focus.

## Sit down in a relaxed spot

There are a lot of various positions that can be used in meditation. The important thing is getting a well comfortable location, and you are okay with it, and you won't strain yourself. The position should be okay that you don't need to prop your body up. There are situations that you can buy a zafu, small floor pillow, among many others to help you prop up. A popular position you can put into practice is the lotus. This is where you sit down on the floor with your back straight, left foot under the right thigh and your right foot layered over the left ankle. In cases where you are meditating for a long time, you have to change how the legs go under the thigh after some time. When meditating on a chair, make sure your back is positioned straight, and your feet placed flat on the ground.

## 2. Accomplishing your meditation

### Time how you breathe

The main objective of any meditative process is by taking your brain off from anything that will distract your thoughts that may come up as you try to center yourself. Breathe out, then slowly and gently breathe in till you feel your lungs are full. You should note the seconds and try to execute the same amount of time to blow out. The duration will mostly depend on how big is your lung, but in general, try to breathe gently. Do this continually to hinder other imaginations from corrupting your mind. You can decide to inhale with your nose and exhale with your mouth. When you want a slow and relaxing meditation, you can try the process 4-7-8 exercise. Breathe out and then close your mouth and breathe in for four seconds, hold on for seven seconds, then you can breathe out for eight seconds.

### Grasp your breath inside for two seconds

You should be attentive to the curve of your breath. This is the curve that changes when you inhale then exhale, then you exhale and inhale. Your breath should not be curved too quickly. This can assist in putting besides a two-second waiting period amid; this is when your lungs are full, and they are empty, thus slowing down the curve.

## Be attentive on your muscle response

You should be thinking about how your body parts will respond to your breathing. Feel your diaphragm, the throat muscles, your shoulders will shift as you breathe in and out to feel your mind. This is not painful stress, but it's just supposed to make you feel how your muscles are stretching in these areas. You can place your hands in the diaphragm for you to explore how the muscles are responding. You can still put your attention on the relaxed body parts. You should put your hands and arms in comfortable positions that do not strain their muscles, and you have to keep focusing there.

## Readdress your traveling mind

You should have a word like "breath" that you can repeat to yourself in cases where you find your soul in wonder world. You should be able to realize that this is a natural occurrence and don't feel demoralized when you are struggling to be attentive. You should have in mind that you need to focus on your breathing patterns.

## Breathing Meditation Exercises

Breathing is vital when you want to achieve being mindful. This is essential because you will have a fantastic feeling of doing yoga, unlike any other aerobics. You will be in control of your breathing as you treat yourself to all the advantages that will come about calmly with a steady flow of fresh air. Oxygen will revitalize you, helps to reset your mind, body, and spirit that will make you have some comfort. When you collectively put this together with meditation and mala beads, then you will have a great feeling of being reborn. All breathing is not created equally. This can be realized in your yoga classes. You should learn how to breathe correctly, and this assists you in how you primarily use the benefits; there are various breathing methods that can be used when you are meditating. Some have been discussed below.

## Communal Yoga Breathing Procedure

When you practice yoga most of the time, then there is a possibility you are aware of this procedure because it is used most through various kinds of yoga. This will help to calm your breathing, and you can enjoy the advantages of taking in fresh oxygen. For you to successfully do this breathing method, you have to follow the directions below.

- Be calm, then inhale
- Pause
- Then gently exhale
- Pause

## Equivalent Breathing

Breathing methods that will assist in calming your brain, body, and soul can be referred to as equal or equivalent breath. This can be the best solution to help in reducing stress, assist in calming your nerves, and make you have an increase in your focus, and you can do this from any place and at any time. There are a few steps that can assist you in breathing method below.

- Breathe in using your nose for a count of four.
- Gently breathe out using your nose for a count of four.

## Count for Four

This is a ubiquitous method for meditating, and all you have to do is count to four. Then you will count backward begin with four timing your breath. Other various numbers will depend on your preferences, and you can see this in the post. Counting to four as been seen as a common denominator. The steps are as shown below.

- Inhale- count one
- Exhale- count two
- Inhale- count three
- Exhale- count four
- Inhale- count three
- Exhale-count two
- Inhale-count one
- Exhale -count two
- Repeat the process

**Abdominal Breathing**

This is considered to be one of the simplest breathing methods at which it is recommended to beginners who want to start meditation.

Nevertheless, this method is possibly used in and outside meditation, and this is because of its real power and helps in the reduction of depression at any given period. You will also spend some moments for you to execute it, this will give you an advantage in any situation where you need to recall yourself. Below are the steps to guide you through.

- Put one hand on your chest

- Take another side and put it on your stomach
- Inhale deeply through the nose
- Feel your hand on your abdomen as it moves as you inflate your diaphragm with oxygen
- Gently exhale

**Stimulating Breath**

It can also be referred to as the bellows breath, and this has the advantage of increasing your attentiveness and energy. You have to practice this severally for you to be perfect when doing it. This will make you feel invigorated, and you will have addiction in the way that it makes you think. Below are the steps.

- With haste, breath in and out using your nose, will little time, balancing time for both inhalation and exhalation. Your target is to have three inhales and exhales every second.
- Do this for five seconds.
- You should increase your time gradually throughout the process till you get to one full minute.

**Alternative Nostril Breathing**

This is a common breathing technique that can be used when meditating, and yoga is the substitute nostril breathing, and this is how it will sound like. When you use this method, then it will allow you to reenergize your brain, physique, and spirit. You can follow the steps below.

- Using your right thumb, plug it into your right nostril
- Breathe in deeply using your left nostril
- Take off your right thumb from your right nose and take your ring finger then plug it into your left nostril
- Gently breath out
- Then repeat the process

**The 4-7-8 Count**

This can also be referred to as the relaxing breath method. It is among the easiest to execute, and as a bonus, the benefits you will have are exponential. This method is the best when it comes to calming down the nervous system; thus, this will assist in tranquilizing the nerves. This can be an excellent method for any person that wants to calm their brains, or if you are suffering from depression or sleep restlessness. Below are the steps on how you can do it.

- Put the tip of your tongue to rest at the top back of your dental formula
- Breathe out profoundly along with a great sigh or whizzing sound
- Shut your mouth and slowly breathe in using your nose in a count of four
- Then take hold of your breathe in a count of seven

- Breathe out deeply and do this in a count of eight, then release a big sigh
- Repeat the process

## Skull Shining Breath

This kind of breathing method is also referred to as Kapalabhati. This is another excellent way that can help you shake off your negative energy and assist you in warming up your brain, body, and spirit. You can use this method in the morning when going to an exam, before you attend your next yoga class, or when meditating. These are the steps that you can use for direction.

- Breath in slowly and let it be deep
- Then quickly breathe powerfully from your diaphragm
- Repeat this process

## Mala Bread Breathing

When you are not good at counting, or you are so much overwhelmed, distracted, stressed to keep counting, mala beads are the perfect explanation. These meditations were used in the tracking of your breath, sans any counting. You have to move your fingers along the mala beads, single for every breath. You need to choose the right mala bread for your purpose; this is because the energy from natural stone can make you have further meditation and be relaxed. The steps to follow are below.

- Choose a specific mala bead precise to your purpose

- Take the mala bead and hold it in your right hand
- Shade it amid your middle and index finger
- Beginning at the guru bead, move your thumb along every smaller bead, breathing in for, respectively.
- Continue doing this for 108 times until you get back to your guru bead

Mala beads are also used in every breathing method that has been mentioned. Breathing Is the most straightforward, most affordable, and inarguably most commanding form of therapy. You are advised to choose a breathing method and some mala beads that will suit your wants and secure the reimbursements of appropriate breathing.

## Easy Breathing Meditation to Improve Mindfulness

With the busy activities of the world, your mind will most of the time be pulled from pillar to post, scattering of your thoughts and feelings, thus parting you stressed, highly strung, and most of the period quite nervous. A lot of people can't even have five minutes of their time to sit down and relax, not yet thirty minutes or more to meditate. For your good, it is advisable to have some minutes daily to cultivate mental spaciousness and enhance a positive mind and body balance. There are various steps that you can use to assist you in emptying your account and get some needed rest.

## Mindful Breathing

You can easily do this exercise anywhere at any time, seated or standing up. You can either choose to sit in a meditating position or not, and there is no big deal. What you are required to do is be still and attentive to your breathe for a minute.

- Begin by breathing in and out gradually, and one should take at least six seconds.
- Inhale through your nose and exhale through your mouth, let your breath to flow naturally in and out of your body.
- Put back your thoughts, all the things that can hold your attention. Let the feelings to rise and fall and be at one with your breathing.
- Persistently be attentive to your breath, put all your mindfulness on its pathway as it gets to your body and as it fills you with life.
- Look at your mindfulness as it operates its way up and out of your mouth, and its vigor dispels into the biosphere.

If, in any case, you thought you wouldn't be able to meditate, then I am sure you are already half the journey. If you had an excellent experience with the relaxing brain exercise, later you can try it two or three times.

## Watchful Observation

This is a very competitive process but very powerful as it will assist you in realizing and escalate the humble fundamentals of your surroundings more thoughtfully. This exercise is supposed to link you with the peace and beauty of nature, something that is missed easily when you are in a hurry in the car or hopping trains as you go to work.

- Take a natural object around your environment and put all your attention viewing it for a minute or more. You can decide to look at a flower, insect, clouds, or the moon.
- You should not engage in anything except the thing you are focusing on. Be calm on watching for a more extended period that you can concentrate.
- Take a look at the object as if it is your first time to see it.
- Try to explore each aspect visually of its formation, then allow yourself to be carried off by its occurrence.
- Let yourself to link with its vigor and its purpose within the natural world.

## Watchful Awareness

This process is designed to enhance a heightened awareness and appreciation of easy day to day tasks and the outcome that they achieve. You should have something in mind that occurs daily or more and should be something that you always take for granted, for instance, opening a door. Any time you are holding the doorknob to open your door, hold on for some moment and be mindful of the place that you are, the feeling you are having, and the route the door will direct you to.

There is a time when you are opening your computer to begin your tasks, take some time to appreciate the hands that made that process successful and the brain that facilitated your understanding of using the computer. The touchpoint cues should not be physical ones. For instance, when you have some negative thoughts, you can decide to take some moments to stop then label your thoughts as helpful and get off the negativity.

You can smell some good food, take your time to stop and appreciate how you are lucky enough to have good food that you can eat and be able to share with your friends and family. Get a touchpoint that can resonate with you, perhaps when you are going through your day to day motions on autopilot. You can choose to take some time to bring about the knowledge of your tasks and the kind of blessings they are enacting in your life.

**Mindful Paying Attention**

With this process, you will be able to open your ears to any sound in a judgmental way. You can also be able to train your mind to be less pulled back by the influence of your previous experiences and presumption. Our past experiences influence a lot of things that we feel. For example, you can dislike a song for some reason of reminding you of your past or sometimes in your life when you had negative encounters. This process has an idea of you listening to some music that is neutral and won't have any impact on you. It should have some present awareness that is unrestricted by presumption. Get some music that you have never heard of before. You can do this by either choosing what you have never listened to in your collection, or you tune into your radio till you get something appealing to your ears.

## Mindful Involvement

This process will help you to bring out contentment in the moments and leak the persistent striving we find ourselves caught up in our day to day basis. You may be anxious to clear up with a daily routine work to try and do something else. You should take that routine and gain its experience fully. For instance, when you are doing some cleaning at your house, be attentive to every detail you are doing. Unlike taking this as a regular task, make a completely new involvement by trying to notice each feature of your actions. When sweeping the floor, try to feel and be the motion, try to sense the muscles when washing the dishes, and create an efficient method to wipe the windows clean. This idea will help you to be creative and develop new practices with your daily familiar program task.

Never be in a hurry to think about finishing the task in your routine, but try to be aware of all the steps and put yourself in the pathway of the development. The activity should be taken beyond routine, and this will be by aligning yourself with it materially, psychologically, and internally.

## Mindful Obligation

When doing this last method, you have to consider five things that you never appreciate daily. The elements can be objects or human beings, and this is upon you. You should have a notepad that will assist you in checking off five when the day is coming to an end. This method will be able to give thanks and escalate the irrelevant things in your life. The things that support your reality but never get second opinions in your wants for great options. For example, electricity will assist in powering your kettle, and the postman will deliver your mail, your clothes will keep you warm, your nostrils will allow you to breathe in flowers in the park, your ears will let you hear the sweet tunes from the birds on the trees. After getting to know the five things, it will be your responsibility to get to know more details about their creation and persistence to honestly escalate the way they are impacting your lifestyle.

# How to Incorporate Breathing to Relax the Body?

Many people think that relaxation is going to flop on your couch and start watching your tv after having a stressful day. This will assist you in reducing stress damages at a tiny percentage. You can do some regular practice that can help you in reducing your daily stress and anxiety. You can improve your sleep anxiety, boost your energy and mood, improve your overall health and wellbeing.

## Breathe Deeply

With full focus and attention, take a deep breath that is simple and will be persuasive to relax your body. You will quickly learn this as it can be practiced anywhere, and it will give you a fast option on how to check your stress levels. This is a cornerstone of various relaxation methods and can be gathered with other elements like music. There are some apps and audios that can take you through the process, and all you require is a quiet place and stretch out.

## Advanced Muscle Easing

This is a two-way step method where you methodically tense and relax various muscle groups in the body. When you practice it more often, you will have been familiar with what tension and body relaxation will feel in different parts of your body. This can assist you to be able to react to the first symptoms of muscular tension that comes with stress. When your body relaxes, your mind too will relax. This type of muscle relaxation can also be combined with deep breathing for further stress reprieve.

## Body Examination Meditation

This kind of meditation will make you attentive to various parts of your body. Similar to progressive muscle relaxation, you can begin with your feet as you work your way up. In this case, you don't tense and relax your muscles, but you have to focus on how every part of your physique feels without tagging the feelings as either good or bad.

## Conception

This is a dissimilarity on old-style contemplation that encompasses understanding a scene in which you sense harmony, permitted to let go all the strain and nervousness. You should be able to get a setting that calms you down, and it can be a tropical beach, a favorite childhood spot, or a silent wooded glen. You can learn this method by practicing on your own with either using an app or audio that you download to guide you through your imagery. At times you can do it in silence or by the assistance of listening aids like fresh music, or sound machine, or possibly recordings that will match your chosen setting. You can select the sound of ocean waves if you decide to go to the beach, for example.

## Self-Massage

By now, you are aware of how a professional massage at a spa or health club can help in the reduction of stress, reduction of pain, and easing of muscle tension. You may not be aware that you can achieve such benefits either at home or work when you put into practice personal massage or trading messages with the people you love or those close to you. You can begin by taking a few minutes to massage yourself at your desk when working; you can do it on your couch after a hectic day, or when in bed to assist you to unwind before you sleep. To enact easing, then you can use aromatic oil, scented lotion, or collectively have an intimate massage with mindfulness or cavernous breathing methods.

# Chapter 4: Abdominal Breathing

*"Take a deep breath and pause for one minute without doing anything! There did you feel the magic?"- Avijeet Das*

Did you know that the average relaxed person takes about 16 breaths per minute? That is about 960 breaths an hour, 23,040 breaths a day, and 8,409,600 a year. But because breathing is an integral part of our existence, we do not give it much thought. But has your breathing been efficient, or have you been breathing through your chest?

Abdominal breathing, also known as diaphragmatic breathing, is a type of breathing that is the basis of all meditation techniques. This type of breathing involves breathing with your belly, and it strengthens the diaphragm. The diaphragm is a dome-shaped skeletal muscle located below your lungs. It contracts (straightens) when you breathe in, allowing the lungs more space to expand. The opposite is the case when you exhale; the diaphragm expands (creating the dome-shape), thereby helping to push the air out, and the lungs contract.

With this technique, you'll learn to regulate your breathing by inhaling slowly and deeply through your nose, holding the breath for 1-2 seconds, then exhaling through your mouth. You can spend 5-10 minutes focusing on your breath either while lying on your back or sitting upright.

## Benefits of Abdominal Breathing

Not only does diaphragmatic breathing act as an anchor for meditation practices, but it also has multiple additional benefits. Diaphragmatic breathing is an innate process, but we get out of the habit when we get older. Listening to or watching a baby breath, we can stand to learn a thing or two. Kids are generally stress-free, so their breathing is more comfortable and more efficient. Today, we have become accustomed to shallow chest breathing because of the constant pressures of life. It is prudent to be aware of the benefits of abdominal breathing and to try and practice it as soon as one is aware of the well-being brought about by deep abdominal breathing. Some of the benefits of this type of breathing include:

- It helps the body to detoxify. This is by stimulating the lymphatic movement, which then flushes the toxins out of the body. These toxins include isoprene, acetone, ethanol, hydrocarbons, and excess carbon dioxide.
- Full oxygen exchange; meaning that the lungs expand fully to allow the carbon dioxide to be expelled, and the oxygen absorbed into the cells.
- This type of breathing slows down the heart rate, thereby stabilizing blood pressure.

- Diaphragmatic breathing also helps to maintain healthy digestion and ease an upset stomach. It does this by stimulating sufficient blood flow to the intestinal tract, keeping the muscles well-functioning. It also prevents intestinal spasms, acid reflux, and bloating.

- Strengthening the diaphragm for people who have chronic obstructive pulmonary disease, where the air is trapped in the lungs, which keeps the diaphragm pressed down, making it work less efficiently. Abdominal breathing helps to strengthen this muscle.

- It helps you relax by lowering the effects of the stress hormone cortisol in your system. This is perhaps the most straightforward use of this breathing exercise. Because reducing stress allows the body organs to work more efficiently, at full capacity.

- This exercise helps you cope with Post Traumatic Stress Disorder (PTSD) symptoms.

- While practicing the breathing relaxation technique, it helps with anger management by releasing the tension that accumulates on the shoulders and back.

- It improves your endurance when undertaking strenuous exercises.

- It reduces your body's demand for oxygen, and you use less energy overall.

- Abdominal breathing has also been proven to be a useful supplemental treatment when it comes to emotional and mental health conditions, including anxiety, stress, and depression. These happen in progression. Therefore, if the problem can be arrested, managed, and treated while it is only just anxiety, it reduces the chances of it progressing to stress. This, in turn, minimizes the possibility of it ever turning to depression. Likewise, if chronic stress can be managed and reversed in good time, in all likelihood, it will not progress to depression. Therefore, learning how to do abdominal breathing at an early stage when anxiety symptoms are presented will ultimately prevent a more than likely unfavorable outcome.

## How It Works

In a nutshell, abdominal breathing involves breathing in through the nose, holding for a few seconds, and breathing out through the mouth. There are various ways in which to practice this, which we will explore below:

### When Lying Down
Lie on your back on a flat surface, with a pillow under your head for support- if possible- and slightly bend your knees. Before you begin the exercise, take stock of your regular breathing pattern. Close your eyes and focus solely on the in-and-out of your breath. Do not engage any other stimuli that are likely to interfere with your breathing, like sounds, smells, etc. How is your breathing?

Is it shallow? Is your belly moving with the breathing rhythm? Are you breathing fast?

When you know how you breathe when you are relaxed on a regular basis, practicing this type of breathing can help promote normal respiration to a more wholesome approach. The next step is to place one hand on your chest and the other on your abdomen, allowing your elbows to rest on the flat surface. When you do this, you will be able to track the movement of your body during the exercise.

Once you are in a comfortable position, breathe in slowly through your nose into the abdomen so that the hand on the belly moves up while the hand on your chest remains as still as possible. Inhale until you can no longer take in more air comfortably.

As you exhale, tighten your abdominal muscles and push out as much air as you can through pursed lips. Exhale until the hand on your belly moves back to its initial position and continue breathing out until you can no longer express air comfortably. Alternatively, you can keep your lips sealed as you exhale through the nose keeping your diaphragm and throat muscles tight.

## While Sitting Upright

As you get better at abdominal breathing, you can practice this exercise while sitting, at any time and place, as opposed to doing it only in your house lying down. For example, you can find some time when you are alone and not very busy, in the office, or at the park, and take ten minutes for this exercise.

Begin in an upright position on a firm, comfortable seat with your shoulders, back, and neck relaxed. Bend your knees to support yourself firmly. Place one hand on your chest and the other below the rib-cage to feel the motion of the diaphragm as you breathe. This hand placement will help you ensure you are breathing correctly. Once your hand placement is in order, concentrate on breathing in and out. The breath in should be slow and through the nose, feel the hand on your stomach rising (moving outward). Contract the abdominal muscles as you exhale through pursed lips and nose until all the air has left the lungs, and the hand on your stomach has resumed the starting position. Notice how the rib-cage and the diaphragm move in a harmonic balance. The movement may be more noticeable while sitting than while lying.

When you have successfully completed the exercise, repeat for another 5-10 minutes, several times throughout the day, if possible. When starting abdominal breathing, it is more convenient to begin while lying down before trying it while sitting. Begin with short periods and increase the length of time as you continue the practice. You can also experiment with different combinations of inhaling and exhale counts or even the depth of each breath. For example, you may want to breathe in for half as long as you exhale- 5-count in, 10-count out.

## Rib Stretch Breathing

Here is how it to do the rib-stretching breathing exercise:

- Stand with your shoulders upright and your back arched
- Exhale fully, to start with a "clean" pair of lungs
- Take a deep, gradual breath in until you cannot comfortably take in any more
- Hold the air in for five seconds
- Exhale slowly through pursed lips

Rib stretching is also another form of abdominal breathing that allows for the full expansion of the lungs and efficient working of the diaphragm. Specifically, you can utilize this breath during yoga to improve your backbends. Since they require a steady lift of the sternum, backbends hold your front ribs in the "breathe in" position while keeping your abs lengthened and generally relaxed. This makes it hard to breathe out because you cannot drive out air from your lungs by bringing down your upper ribs or by firmly contracting your abdominal muscles. The less air you exhale, the less fresh air you take in, you, therefore, end up with an imbalanced ratio of oxygen to carbon dioxide in the body; the carbon dioxide is more. That is one explanation for why individuals tire while doing backbend exercises.

**Numbered Breathing**

Numbered breathing is especially desirable for one who wants to gain control over their breathing patterns. Below is an illustration of how you may go about it:

1. Stand upright, close your eyes, and keep still.
2. Take a slow deep breath until you cannot comfortably take in any more air.
3. Breath out forcibly, until all air from your lungs has been emptied.
4. Remember to close your eyes through the process. Now inhale as you picture the first step. Hold the air in your lungs for a while, then breath out.
5. Inhale again as you picture the second step. Hold breath as you silently count one to 3, then exhale again.
6. Repeat these steps until you've reached a holding count of 8.
7. Eight is the threshold for most, but if you feel comfortable, you may count higher.

## A Meditation Technique

Using abdominal breathing as the base of any meditation, you may now want to exercise this skill in a meditation pose of your choice. For example, you may choose to lie down in what is called the Savanna pose. On a flat surface or rug, place your hands on your side with the palms facing up. Note that we do not track the movement of the abdomen and chest in this technique because we have already mastered diaphragmatic breathing. With your hands on your side, take in a slow, deep breath for five counts in-and-out, and remain mindful of your breathing. With every breath, notice the areas of your body that are holding tension and feel the pressure leaving your body with each exhale.

During meditation, breathing becomes the focus of the exercise. Let your mind concentrate on the movement of the body as you draw in air, notice how much air is coming in, and how your muscles are responding to it. The main object of focus remains as the influx of air. This breathing technique engages the muscles in the lower back and at the core, allowing more stability. This stability is essential for meditation poses.

Practicing deep abdominal breathing before meditation helps us experience a more meaningful activity riddled with purpose. When we are able to dedicate our attention to one thing for a prolonged duration, then that means that we are training our minds to limit the scope of attention. Studies have shown that diaphragmatic breathing increases the blood flow in the prefrontal cortex, making our thoughts more focused, clear, and conscious. This exercise improves self-control. However, the objective during meditation is to relax the concentration on breathing and increase the duration of mindfulness meditation.

Another study reasoned that diaphragmatic breathing, through the actuation of the parasympathetic sensory system, diminishes glycemia, increases insulin, and lessens receptive oxygen metabolites- reducing oxygen demand in the body. Moreover, gradual, deep breathing upgrades respiratory system capacity and enhances cardiorespiratory wellness and respiratory muscle tenacity.

Creating a routine is an excellent practice to start and maintain the breathing exercise. Do not worry that you may be doing it incorrectly at the beginning because this may cause additional cortisol production. During practice, focus on the movement and sounds of your body as you breathe. Do it at least twice a day at the same time every day to enforce the habit of deep breathing. And never do it for less than five minutes each day. Because we are building strength and endurance, we should aim at pacing ourselves and not allowing ourselves to slack. The exercise also strengthens the intention of meditation by helping one to keep focused and grounded.

## Impulse Control

Impulse control is simply defined as the ability to think before acting. It is achieved by developing the requisite skills to forego an immediate desire and wait for a later reward, also known as delayed gratification. Impulse control is most effective when learned in childhood. This is when we learn to take turns, especially with the things we like the most, and it is also at this early stage in life we learn how to share what we have with our friends and to partake gratefully in what we do not have. Additionally, we learn how not to overreact when we are frustrated or angry.

Diaphragmatic breathing is an excellent aid when learning impulse control. It helps us to regulate ourselves by checking our nervous systems and helps us to master how to hold a safe emotional space. A breathing exercise that can be used by youngsters and adults alike to control negative impulses like lashing out by aggressive behaviors such as hitting or screaming is the "Hissing Breath." You practice this by taking a deep breath through the nose, counting to five, and then exhaling slowly while making a long hissing sound, like a deflating balloon. Repeat this a few times, and there will be a marked improvement in your emotional disposition. You can do it as many times as you need until you feel that you are in control again, and all the pent-up anger or frustration has worked itself out of your system.

## Propagation of Abdominal Breathing

Fortunately, the air we breathe is virtually free of charge. When an opportunity presents itself to make use of this resource more efficiently, one should be all the more eager to embrace the opportunity and improve their general well-being. There is supporting evidence that abdominal breathing has tremendous physical and psychological effects on our bodies. With this in mind, we should aim to bring our breathing as close as possible to perfection, and also teach and train others to do the same.

Key to this would be maybe to train the pre-teens and teens, who are likely to be experiencing the first few stressful situations in life, including a myriad of physiological changes. Perhaps if we do our best to keep them well balanced through effective breathing techniques, we will be helping them to cope better with life's challenges, turning out better-functioning adults for the future. When we have implemented such a program or structure, we can be sure to have made a positive impact on posterity.

# Chapter 5: Vipassana Meditation

*"Life is a dance, and mindfulness is witnessing that dance."- Amit Ray*

Vipassana means seeing things as they are. Vipassana meditation is a way in which you can self-transform yourself through self-observation. This kind of meditation focuses on the deep interconnection between your mind and body. You can directly experience this interconnection by paying a lot of disciplined attention to the physical sensations forming the life of your body. These sensations continuously interconnect and conditions the state of your mind.

It is this observation-based, self-exploratory meditation, which dissolves your mental impurities for you to achieve a balanced mind full of nothing but love and compassion.

Through vipassana meditation, the prevailing scientific laws that operate your thoughts, feelings, judgments, and sensations are made more manifest. Through direct experience, you become more aware of how you grow or regress, how you produce suffering, or free yourself from it, and thus, it helps you increase your awareness, and become non-delusional. This meditation also helps you to increase your self-control and peace of mind.

## The Origin

Vipassana meditation was rediscovered by Gotama Buddha more than 2500 years ago. It gained popularity to become one of India's most ancient meditation techniques which are relevant up to date. Gotama Buddha taught and popularized the vipassana meditation as one of the universal remedies for all kinds of ills that people faced at the time. He aimed at empowering people to use this technique to eradicate all their mental impurities to achieve happiness and liberation.

Since the time of Gotama Buddha, vipassana mediation has been handed down from generation to generation by a chain of committed and dedicated teachers. The current teacher is an Indian born man called S.N Goenka. In S.N Goenka was born and raised in Burma, Myanmar, in the early 1920s. He recalls that while living there, he was lucky to learn Vipassana from his teacher Sayagi U Ba Khin. After being trained by his teacher for over a decade, Goenka settled in India and dedicated much of his time and effort to teaching Vipassana meditation from the year 1969.

Since then, he has taught hundreds of thousands of people this unique meditation technique from all regions and races of the world.

In 1982 Goenka began appointing his assistants to help him meet the growing demand for the vipassana courses.

## Vipassana Training Course: How Long Does It Take, And What Does It Involve?

Vipassana meditation technique is taught as a ten-day residential course in which you follow a strict prescribed code of discipline. Apart from following the code of discipline, you should also learn the basics of the method and do sufficient practice on it for you to experience beneficial results.

You should note that the course demands a lot of hard work and commitment from you, and as such, you must be willing to go the extra mile if you are to benefit from it.

In the first step of the course, you are taught how to abstain from killing, stealing, engaging in sexual activity, speaking falsely, and from all forms of intoxicants. This is a simple code of moral conduct that helps you calm your mind to enable it to perform well the function of self-observation.

You are then taught how to develop a mastery over your mind by learning to fix your attention on your breathing. You are taught how to be attentive to the actual reality of the flow of your breathing. How you master your breath as it enters and leaves your nostrils is one of the critical skills of vipassana mediation you must possess.

Other aspects of the course include learning how to calm your mind and remain focused to observe your body's sensations and react to them accordingly. You are also taught how to meditate on loving-kindness to achieve purity.

The entire practice of vipassana is mental training. Just as you use physical exercises to improve your health, vipassana also makes use of mental activities to develop a healthy, focused mind. The subsequent teachers of this meditation technique go to great lengths in preserving the method in its most original and authentic from.

## What Are the Requirements for One to Be Accepted in The Training?

The mediation technique is not taught commercially; instead, the teachers offer the training freely to whoever is interested. Besides, there are no religious, racial, cultural, or gender requirements for you to train in vipassana techniques.

Because the course doesn't charge even to cover the cost of food and accommodation, all the expenses are met through donations. Most of those donations come from the people who previously trained in the course and experienced significant benefits. Perhaps, they are touched to allow others to experience the benefits too, and that is why they donate generously.

## How Long Should You Wait to Experience the Benefits of Vipassana?

You should expect to experience the results gradually over time. If you are assuming all your problems to be solved within the ten-day training period, then you are unrealistic. However, you can learn the essentials of vipassana within the period to apply them throughout your everyday living experiences.

Remember, the more you practice the technique, the higher the benefits you experience. Over time you will ultimately gain freedom from your misery and achieve your goal of full liberation. You can also expect to achieve sound and vivid results, even within the short ten-day training period.

## What Happens During the Ten-Day Silent Vipassana Meditation Period?

Vipassana is intended to be a non-religious and non-dogmatic meditation. Its views and principles are designed not to conflict with any religious beliefs you subscribe to.

The idea behind the vipassana retreat is for you to sit around all day and learn how to sharpen your awareness of what is going on inside your body and mind using your physical sensations. You can choose any of the various settings which vary in lengths.

There are vipassana retreats that last from 3 days to 3 months. However, the first ten days are the most crucial. Each of the ten days involves 10 hours of serious meditation.

The following is a current schedule you are expected to follow for each of the 10-day meditation periods.

**4:00 am**- The wake-up bell goes off. You are expected to wake up and prepare for the meditation sessions promptly

**4:30 am to 6:30 am**- you carry out your meditation in silence

**6:30 am to 8: 00 am**- you undertake breakfast

**8:30 am to 11:00 am**- you resume your meditation in silence

**11:00 am to 1:00 pm**- you take a one-hour lunch break

**1:00 pm to 5: 00 pm**- you undertake your afternoon meditation in silence

**5:00 pm to 6: 00 pm**- you break your afternoon mediation to take a one-hour tea break

**6:00 pm to 7:00 pm**- you resume your meditation

**7:00 pm to 8:15 pm**- you attend a conventional lecture

**8:30 pm to 9:00 pm**- you undertake the last meditation exercise of the day

**10:00 pm- lights out-**You go to bed.

If you follow the above schedule strictly, then you will get yourself more than ten hours of meditation daily. If you can consistently meditate for the 10 hours each day, then at the end of the ten days, you will have meditated for over 100 hours.

Most of your meditation is loosely structured, and thus you can choose to carry on with it in the main hall with others or in your room alone. If you decide to mediate in the hall, you will be assigned your spot and given a mat to sit on.

Later on, you will also be given a small cell which you can make use of during your meditation period. The cells are quieter and can remind one of being in solitary confinement. Although you may find it awkward staying in one initially, you will soon find comfort and a sense of tranquility once you have familiarized yourself with the inside surroundings.

You should also take note of the three-hour-long mandatory meditation period. These are the 8 am to 9 am from, the 2:30 pm to 3:30 pm and 6 pm to 7 pm meditation periods. In all these mandatory periods, you are expected to stay in the hall with the rest of the trainees.

During the lecture portion, you can expect to watch recorded videos of some of the influential vipassana speakers, including a video of S.N Goenka. Goenka is an influential meditation teacher who has been very instrumental in the popularization of vipassana across the entire globe. He majorly emphasizes the non-religious and scientific teachings that help solve other people's problems.

The lecture portion also seeks to provide context for what you have been working on during the meditation exercise of that particular day. It also aims to set the stage for the meditation exercise s of the following day.

## Day 0 (Day Zero)

## The Noble Silence

You are expected to travel from your location to one of the vipassana centers across the world once you register for the training. The organizers have a sound coordination system to help you coordinate a ride-share with some of the meditators traveling to the same destination.

Once you show up at the meditation center, you are expected to introduce yourself formally. You are also allowed to mingle and interact with the other meditators. You will be surprised to find people who have done several sittings before, some even for more than ten sessions.

On the evening of day 0, you are given a very light dinner. You are then led to the main hall where everyone is assigned their particular spot to sit and meditate on. You conduct a brief meditation on your assigned place that day before you are assisted in making a noble silence.

The noble silence is simply a vow of silence for 10 days. It means you maintain a state of silence for the next ten days during your meditation period. At first, you may find keeping this vow a challenge, but you will soon realize it is by far the least challenging part of the whole training.

Being a social being, you will try to make eye contact or communicate with others using gestures; however, even nonverbal communication is highly discouraged during the entire period of your meditation.

The reason why the organizers insist on silence is that you tend to be more focused and attentive to what you are experiencing inside your body when in a calm, serene environment. Silence also prevents you from comparing your meditations with those of others or judging your personal experiences against theirs. Silence is, therefore, a key to making the whole experience effective.

## Separation of Men and Women

Day one also will see you being separated depending on your gender. Men and women are separated and given different sleeping facilities. You are also expected to take your meals in separate areas. Moreover, the grounds where men and women are allowed to walk in are also distinct.

However, the only place where the male and female share is the meditation hall. But you are expected to stay on separate sides of the hall. There is no physical divider or a wall between you and the members of the opposite sex, and thus you can still get a view of them whenever you feel like. However, you should be careful not to make eye contact with them.

Although it may appear archaic, it works in making you focus much on your meditation exercises. It also helps you avoid unnecessary distractions and temptations, such as physical attraction, flirtations, or trying to communicate with your partner.

# The Other Forbidden Things During Your Meditation Period

1. You are not allowed to use your cell phone during the entire period. You are then expected to give up your phone at the beginning.

2. You are not also allowed to read or write anything. If you carried your journal book along, you are also expected to hand it in for safekeeping until you are through with the training

3. You are not allowed to use any intoxicants during your meditation period. However, tea and coffee are freely provided for those who need to shoot up their caffeine levels.

4. Lying is strictly discourage. However, the fact that you are not allowed to talk makes this one of the easy rules to follow.

5. You are not also allowed to kill. You are not allowed to undertake any killing as well as any emotional killing physically. You let your emotions to flow freely without suppressing them

6. Stealing is also strictly forbidden. Should you take anything that doesn't belong to you without permission will result in instant expulsion from the training program.

## The Expected Meditation Pains

When you sit for ten hours a day, you may experience a level of pain, even if you are an experienced meditator. Part of the training requires you to observe your pain and discomfort to develop a sense of mental calm and composure whenever you are under any pressure out there in your real world.

The pain of sitting for long hours is real, and although you will start with a mat and a single cushion, by the end of the ten days, you will probably have created an elaborate set up for yourself consisting of several cushions arranged in different ways that make you comfortable.

If you find it hard to withstand the pain, you can request for a plastic chair which the organizers will readily provide. The plastic chair, however, will significantly increase your chances of falling asleep while you are meditating.

Another viable option is using the meditation bench. The advantage with the meditation bench is that it reduces the pressure and the strain which you feel, especially on your upper thighs and back whenever you sit for too long. Meditation bench is greatly encouraged if you find sitting for long periods to be a challenge.

**Key Insights You Can Learn from Vipassana Meditation**

Once you are through with your training, there are some key insights you ought to pick and incorporate into your daily living. These include:

I.    What causes most of the human suffering is aversion and cravings. Whenever you crave for something which you can't get, such as money or love, you will end up feeling miserable. You are also likely to be miserable when you fail to evade uncomfortable situations that cause pain, boredom, or hopelessness.

II.    It is hard for humans to satisfy their cravings or aversion. Even when you succeed in satisfying them, they are immediately replaced with new cravings and aversions. For example, that good feeling you get after getting a pay rise doesn't last for long. You will soon find that the money is not enough, and you will start craving for even a higher paycheck.

III.    Another insight is that the world you live in is continuously changing. Nothing is permanent. What is relevant today is useless tomorrow. The same applies to our bodies. They age every second, and you are a different person each time you wake up. This is the fact which you are most likely to forget or ignore.

IV.    Although you understand the things mentioned above intellectually or conceptually, you fail to understand the actual and tangible experiences taking place in your body. In vipassana, you are encouraged to use your body as a framework through which you seek to understand the world better.

V. Another critical insight is the fact that every part of your body is continually experiencing sensory stimulation at all times, but your conscious mind prevents you from being aware of them, especially the small sensations. Your conscious mind only allows you to be mindful of the significant sensations such as pains and discomfort.

VI. You can train your conscious mind to be more aware of the small and subtle sensations which continuously go on in your body. However, this training takes a lot of time and practice.

VII. Your subconscious mind continually responds to the subtle non-conscious sensations at all times of the day. That is why when a fly land on your face while you are sleep, your body will swat it away without you even being aware it was there in the first place. And when you have any itchy part, you tend to scratch it even without thinking.

VIII. Another critical insight is that you can separate a sensation from how you automatically respond to it. For example, if you ignore an itchy part, you will tend to get more comfortable observing it. This gives you the realization that all stimulus will eventually go away on their own. This is what is referred to as the law of nature in vipassana.

IX. It is also possible to separate the sensation of pain from the suffering you associate with it. This means that you can feel pain without being bothered by it. That is why studies have revealed that people with chronic pain suffer because of their anticipation of future pain; for example, they keep thinking how much their leg will hurt when they stand up. The expectation will eventually activate the parts of the brain matrix in their brains. This is the location where pain processes take place. Vipassana meditation is beneficial for people suffering from chronic pain conditions.

X. You are not addicted to things. Rather you are addicted to the sensations which those things produce. If you are an alcoholic, you are not addicted to alcohol, but to the sensation you get once you are drunk.

XI. Your mind spends a lot of time reliving past events or imagining future events because those thoughts produce subtle but pleasant sensations in your body.

## The Benefits of Vipassana Meditation

• Vipassana empowers you to detach yourself from material things and helps you to control your cravings to do certain things. You also have control over the desire to indulge in certain habits that you usually find hard resisting.

- The ten-day retreat can help you quit your smoking or drinking habits. Remember, no intoxicants are allowed while you are undertaking your retreat.

- Through the meditation exercises, you will be able to gain better concentration in whatever you do. Students who practice vipassana meditation have seen their academic performance improve significantly.

- Vipassana meditation has also helped so many people overcome their mental problems such as stress, depression, anxiety, and many more.

- It also helps you to increase your self-awareness. You will be more aware of the positive and negative aspects of your personality and life in general. The ten days of meditation will afford you a lot of time for self-reflection.

- It also helps you to remain equanimous no matter the heat you are experiencing. Equanimity means you are ready to accept all outcomes, whether they are good or bad. You won't cling to pleasant experiences, and you won't avert bad ones.

- It will also help you acknowledge the impermanence of the things and people in your life. You will realize everything grows old and eventually die, and therefore, there is no need in clinging on to them. You will tend to accept things as they are because you are receptive to change.

- The noble silence will help you detox from life. You eliminate life's distractions to focus on meditations.
- The pain, silence, and extended period of sitting will offer you a chance to appreciate all the great things and people life has to offer. You will strive to find happiness from the blessings you have rather than looking out there for the unknown pleasures of the world.

# Chapter 6: Chakra Healing

*Every man is the builder of a temple called his body, nor can he get off by hammering marble instead. -- Henry David Thoreau*

Chakra translates to' a wheel 'or 'a disk; it is referred to as "the spinning wheel of light." It is because chakras relate to the balance of the seven distinct energy centers in the body that start at the bottom of the spine and end at the top of the head. All these core energy centers correspond differently to your mental and physical aspects. Chakra, therefore, has a direct relationship to the emotional and physical wellness of a being to continue in a healthy lifestyle; thus, blocked chakras lead to physical illness and sensitive strains. It is, therefore, ideal for each person to learn to identify the blockages and imbalances in their chakra systems to apply appropriate realignment practices. It will make them aware of the habits and choices contributing to the inequity and thus build new habits and make conscious decisions that enable a balanced chakra for a soaring life.

Chakra healing is an esoteric medieval era theory that revolves around the psychological and psychic centers that emerged across Indian traditions. The Hindu and Buddhists are well known for the practice of the chakra healing, which ensured a balance in physical, emotional, energetic, mental, and spiritual aspects of their lives.

## Types of Chakras

Exercises help to locate each chakra, for proper awareness and control of each, thus enabling proper alignment as well as rebalance of the seven core energies. Each of the seven is represented by a distinctive symbol, color, and element, which helps the individuals to pick out representative objects for manifestation and mediation work. The seven chakras have distinct locations and are associated with different emotional and behavioral issues during balance as well as when they are blocked. Each is thus to be uniquely handled during meditation to bring out the desired balance in the individual.

## 1. The Root Chakra (Muladhara)

Muladhara referred to as "root support" or "base. "The root chakra sits at the bottom of your spine and is highly associated with issues connected to financial security, safety, stability, physical health, family, and survival. A well-balanced root chakra gives one a sense of protection required to explore and experiment with new things in life, be it a change of jobs, a move to a different city, a new business risk you will always feel ready. It is due to the feeling of stability, relaxation, which makes one comfort-table with their lives. The root chakra is located at the base of the spine. It has a symbol of four petals. The root chakra represents foundation and security. It is associated with the color red, is a solid color, and brings to mind feelings of survival, instinct, vigilance, and alertness. Its element is the earth, thus promoting a sense of being grounded and connected more to nature.

## Physical, emotional, and behavioral issues associated with the blocked root chakra

The blocked root chakra causes one to feel sore on the lower back, digestive discomforts, lethargy, pain in the legs experience rather cold extremities, as well as have low energy levels, thus feeling less indulgent to the physical activities assigned to them. It will cause individuals to be less productive in their areas of duty if they are employed. Besides, they are easily distracted from their primary responsibilities as well as developing truant behavior or chronic absenteeism to avoid being engaged in any form of activity. If they are students, they will be tempted to spend most of their time sleeping due to the general body exhaustion and fail to tend to their studies leading to poor grades.

As the physical signs settle in, the emotional issues, continue to take a toll. One will often feel threatened or unsafe, anxious, and panicky thus panic attacks that is hyperventilation or a racing heart which will be as a result of the individual's basic survival needs lacking or the primary source of the needs (money, food, clothing, shelter) being cut off. The behavior will change radically as the individual will more often be preoccupied with worries; thus, a manifestation of paranoia will be evident. Moreover, there will be a constant lack of concentration as the thoughts of how to solve their needs occupy them for the better part. The individuals will also tend to feel inadequate, therefore continually speaking negatively about themselves and others. Low self-esteem will be evident as they think they are not worthy or even good enough for the task assigned. Indecisiveness will be apparent in most instances since they are afraid of making the wrong decision that will cost them their security. As all these behaviors continue to manifest, the individual will lack a good relationship with food since they are regularly preoccupied with other thoughts that make them not need for food.

## Root chakras healing

Opening each chakra has its physical, emotional, and behavioral benefits. Therefore, giving a balance to the root chakra can have profound benefits on how you feel. You can significantly improve your self-confidence, your appetite, as well as your decision-making ability as you will now explore in touch with your emotions, giving you a sense of relaxation that enables you to engage in fun and more playful activities. This general sense of stability is basically enough to make all aspects of your life illuminate with positivity as opposed to the previous situation when your root chakra was blocked.

## Techniques for unblocking root chakra

By either wearing as a form of jewelry or holding the four unique stones associated with the opening of the blocked root chakra, one can realign or unblock the root chakra.

These four stones are;

- Red jasper associated with balance; thus, it is the most appropriate stone to wear or hold if you are battling erratic mood swings.
- Red carnelian is associated with cleansing, strength, and bravery; therefore, if you are looking forward to leaving your comfort zone, overcoming fear, this is the stone to hold.

- Obsidian is a black stone that is meant to protect you from harm, thus giving you a sense of comfort as you shift to a greater understanding of security wear it.
- Bloodstone is green in color dawned with red spots. This stone will push away negativity, thus increasing an individual's confidence in whatever they undertake.

**Meditation and yoga techniques**

Regular meditation focused on a specific area of the body will also enhance the rebalancing of the root chakra apart from the above unique stones. Use these meditation techniques to open blocked root chakra;

1. Sit with your spine straight and shoulders back. Close your eyes, relax your muscles as you breathe in through the nose and exhale through the mouth.
2. In the same position, focus your attention on the root support.
3. The color of the root chakra is red, thus picture a red glow at the base of your spine. The whole area will feel warm and relaxed, maintain this position for five minutes.
4. Slowly open your eyes after the five minutes have elapsed.

**Foods and diet enhancing root chakra balance**

Apart from meditation, yoga, and the stones, one can also use these foods linked to the root chakra to realign their chakra. Organic foods are excellent in the opening of the root chakra as they align with our tribal roots. Protein-rich foods are functional, too, as they give one a boost in physical and emotional strength. Red foods can enrich you with vitamin C, and they are associated with the chakra's red color, thus having a direct effect on the root chakra.

Root vegetables are dug from the ground, which too, has a direct relation to the chakra's element, which is earth. Therefore, these beets, potatoes, garlic are going to help in realigning and balancing of the root chakra. A healthy diet that has reduced sugars, salts, and saturated fats, as well as increased intake of fruits and vegetables will have a positive impact on your vibrations and the alignment of your root chakra. In addition to all the techniques applied to open up blocked root chakra, the power of the tongue also comes into play as you have to keep making statements of positive affirmations as a way of enhancing the other techniques in case, you sense a block. For example; "I am happy" "I am safe," "I will never lack anything."

## 2. Sacral Chakra (Svadhishthana)

Svadhishthana, "Save" meaning self "shthana" meaning place.it is situated at the lower level of the sacrum marking the second level of development towards purity. The sacral brings about the creative expression of emotions in matters related to sexuality and relationships when, in balance, it leaves one feeling confident, stimulated, full of ideas to make dynamic and significant changes in the way they live. The sacral chakra is located in the middle of the abdomen just below the belly button.

It has a symbol of six petals, each petal representing; anger, hatred, jealousy, cruelty, desire, pride. It is associated with creativity, emotions, and sexual health. Its color is orange. Orange being a creative and energizing color that can bring feelings of passion, pleasure, and purity this, in return, will promote feelings of safety and abundance. Its element is water.

## Physical, emotional, and behavioral issues associated with the blocked sacral chakra

The sacral chakra is blocked due to several problems that affect relationships (when one is rejected) and sexuality (sexual incompatibility) and creativity (failure to achieve skeptical works of arts as desired or rejection of the works). When one has blocked their sacral chakra, they tend to have bladder discomfort, severe allergies, reduced libidos, as well as reduced energy levels. As the imbalance continues to takes a twist in emotional wellness, the individual will develop feelings of guilt about past events in their life, jealousy, reduced or lack of creativity, irritability, lack of interest in any fun activities, and low self-worth. Addictive behavior will set in as the individual seeks to find solace and identity in alcohol, drugs which will impact negatively on their finances, and some may develop gambling problems as they try to crawl out of the deep financial strains. Others will tend to overeat and overspend as they find a place to channel their emotions.

## Sacral chakra healing

Developing a balanced and realignment of the sacral will help overcome blocks in creativity and vitality; thus, one can let go of feelings of guilt, engage with others freely, boost self-esteem as well as develop healthier ways of regulating with negative emotions. Once you have achieved the balance, you will experience joy as well as profound inspirations that will make you feel that your problem-solving skills have been redefined.

## Sacral chakra healing stones

These are stones with an old link and can be held, carried, or worn as jewelry. These healing stones are;

- Orange calcite is orange in color and has the power to reunite body and mind due to its ability to enhance creativity.
- Moonstone comes in many colors with the preference being peach as it stimulates the brain producing loving energy and reduces worry.
- Carnelian has an intrinsic link to your creativity and artistry. Its color is red-brown hue.
- Citrine is golden yellow, ideal if you have reduced confidence and jealousy as it will help increase your self-esteem.

## Meditation and yoga techniques

Meditation involves a visualization component that helps to unblock the power center at your navel. Its steps are;

1. Sit with your back straight and shoulders out in a quiet place.
2. Take ten slow deep breaths, inhale through the nose and exhale through the mouth.
3. Visualize a spinning orange circle of light in the location of your sacral chakra.
4. Do this for at least five minutes
5. Foods and diet for sacral chakra wellness

## 3. Solar Plexus Chakra (Manipura)

Manipura "mani" meaning jewel "Pura" meaning place or city.it is associated with the kidneys and the stomach diaphragm in the human body. The solar brings out an individual's sense of personal power, personal will own truth, sense of identity as well as moral ethics, and integrity. The solar plexus is located around the stomach between the navel and the lower part of the chest at the top of your abdomen. Its symbol has a lotus of ten petals; these represent the ten pranas, the vital forces which control and nourish the functions of the human body... It is associated with confidence and individuality. Its color is yellow. Yellow as a color brings to mind thoughts and feelings of courage, optimism, and self-esteem. It is an emotional color, as well. Its element is fire, and it manifests in the body as heat in the solar plexus. It, therefore, controls the energy balance to strengthen and consolidate our health.

## Psychological, physical, and emotional issues

Imbalances of the solar plexus will cause the individual to more often not be in touch with their inner person; thus, will have problems with those in authority as they tend to overstep boundaries due to their constant feeling that they are always in control. When in authority, individuals with an imbalance of solar plexus will tend to misuse the power given to them by making their subjects feel unappreciated. They can also be manipulative; therefore, will tend always to shift circumstances to their favor. These individuals experiencing blockages will also make plans but will not make an effort to turn them to reality. As a consequence, they will lack a clear direction, purpose, and even ambition. They will also tend to look at life as a glass half empty instead of a glass half full.

## Healing of the solar plexus

When one is experiencing the realignment and balance of the solar plexus, they can find a balance in their power, and relationships with others are in great shape. It, therefore, enables them to be more assertive in what they want of themselves and others. the individuals are also able to exert their will without hurting or being manipulative to those involved. Besides, they have a harmonious relationship existing with their surroundings.

**Healing stones**

The stones are shaped into gems and worn as jewelry, carried around in the pockets, and touched every time one feels as if they are going to have a block of the solar chakra. During meditation and yoga, one can hold the stones in their hands as this exercise is done in a fixed position. The rocks that help in realignment of the solar plexus are;

- Amber, which exists in a yellowish-green color and promotes confidence as it increases mental clarity so that one can develop a balance.
- Citrine has a pale-yellow color that increases an individual's empowerment.
- Lemon quartz is yellow and helps enhance optimism so that the individual can make reality their plans.

## 4. Heart Chakra (Anahata)

The heart chakra is found directly above the heart. It has a symbol of a lotus with twelve petals inside the smoky region of an intersection of two triangles. This symbol represents the union of male and female. Its color is green, and the element is air.it manifests itself in the individual's life with issues of giving and receiving unconditional love for self as well as others, healing, forgiveness, and compassion.

## Physical, emotional, and behavioral issues associated with the heart chakra imbalance

Dealing with an ending relationship or unreciprocated love, grief, a loss can trigger an imbalance of the heart chakra. Physically the individual will exhibit restlessness, insomnia, increased blood pressure, decreased immune system function as well as lack of empathy this will be as a result of one being unable to consolidate relationships with others not necessarily the romantic relationships but also friendships. Emotionally the individual will find it hard to trust others will be highly irritable even by the minor things due to the lack of patience.

## Healing your heart chakra

An open-heart chakra enables one to understand their own emotional needs as well as meet their individual needs. It will, therefore, put them in a better position for them to be able to extend the same to their significant other (spouse) or even the friends. To realign your heart chakra, therefore, you need to bring your mind body and spirituality in harmony.

## Heart chakra stones

These stones can be worn as earrings, bracelets necklaces, or held in the hand as one is meditating. The stones are;

- Jade is a precious heart stone associated with emotional healing and balance, thus appropriate when one is dealing with loss or psychological injury.

85

- Green calcite is used to absorb negativity, thus an excellent stone when one is struggling to recover from emotional fatigue.
- Green aventurine is directly linked to vitality, energy, and inspirations, thus suitable to one who is recovering from emotional roadblocks as it can soothe calm the emotions.
- Rose quartz as the name suggests this stone is pink in color; unlike all the others that are green, it is associated with regaining the general emotional balance.

## 5. Throat Chakra (Vishuddha)

It is located in the middle of the throat. It has a symbol of sixteen petals that have a triangle pointing downwards in the middle. Its color is blue. Blue is an intellectual color it is associated with feelings of intelligence and being trustworthy. Its element is air.

## Physical, emotional, and behavioral issues

Blocked throat chakra mainly revolves around the issues to do with an individual not being able to communicate their feelings to be understood and their needs met by the others. Physical problems will manifest themselves in the form of a sore throat, erratic fluctuations in hormone levels as well as stiff neck. Psychological and behavioral will come off as; lack of connection with one's purpose in life, lack of control over one's speech, shyness, excess fear of speaking to people, chronic liar, unable to keep secrets as well as not being able to keep promises. An individual will also experience difficulty expressing their needs to others and will sometimes feel as if people do not understand them. They will also feel as if they are being ignored because nobody knows who they are.

Healing throat chakra Positive affirmation statements by the individual are also part of the healing process. Some of the affirmations are:

"I am a clear speaker."
"When I express myself, others understand me."
"I will not be afraid to be heard."

Healing of the throat chakra can sound complicated due to it's associated with speech. However, it only needs constant exerting and constant personal affirmation statements by the individual. Healing throat chakra enables one to express themselves freely thus giving them the power to live a more authentic life due to the end of strained personal and work relationships.

**Throat chakra stones**
The stones can be carried around, or they can be worn; they can as well be held in hand during the meditation or yoga. The stones are;

- Lapuzi lazuli is a stone associated with truth; thus, it is very appropriate to one who is working towards living an honest life.

- Aquamarine represents courage and acceptance; therefore, best recommended to one who is striving to achieve communication in close relationships.
- Amazonite protects one from negativity, so one can wear it if they experience the fear of judgment, which keeps them from speaking their truth.
- Turquoise generally helps boots individual confidence in communication.

**Heart chakra foods and diets**

What you feed on has a significant impact on these energy centers. Therefore, when you feel blocked or unsettled at heart chakra, these are the foods you should consume:

- Green foods, as anything green in color, is associated with having a positive influence on the heart chakra, like the spinach, limes, bell peppers kales.
- Warm soups help replenish the immune system as they have anecdotal evidence, which will make them promote recovery from illness as well as emotional difficulties.
- Foods that are rich in vitamin C, include fresh fruits that can be blended for a smoothie to sooth and open that blockage on the heart chakra.

## 6. Third Eye Chakra (Ajna)

The third eye chakra is located in the center of the eyebrow. It has a symbol of a lotus flower with two petals. Inside the pericarp is a white moon, six faces, and six arms holding a skull book, drum, and a rosary. The triangle facing downwards together with the lotus flower cab symbolizes wisdom. Its color is indigo; being a pure color brings to mind thoughts and feelings of psychic power and peace. Its element is light and is associated with conscious, perspective as well as intuition.

## Physical, psychological, and behavioral issues

Triggers of third eye imbalance will differ according to an individual; there are those whose imbalance will occur as a result of someone demeaning what they do for a living. For others, it will be as a consequence of loss of job, divorce, death, illness given to how sensitive you are to the worth of life. Physical issues associated with the imbalance of the third eye chakra include severe headaches, eye discomfort, back, and leg pain. An individual will get to appoint here; they will feel that they have got no significant contribution to this life. Also, they will think that what they do is not fulfilling, develop indecisiveness as well as constant paranoia at anything that threatens their safety

## Healing third eye chakra

An open third eye chakra is a key to a joyous life. A finely tuned intuition will give one a significant drift toward the right opportunities as one can make sound and profound judgment on considerate life issues. Having an open third eye chakra will always give you a great sense of the bigger picture.

**Healing stones**

The healing stones can be carried around and held on to when one requires the help of the third eye, worn or held on to during meditation and yoga exercises. Some the best third eye chakra stones include:

- Purple fluorite is an ideal stone to an individual making a significant decision and wants to push away irrelevant distractions since it promotes a sharpened intuition.
- Amethyst represented wisdom in some ancient communities and was used as a relief for headaches.
- Black obsidian is a stone that promotes a balance between emotion and reason to enable one to make a decision based on logic and not their present emotional state.

**7. Crown Chakra (Sahasrara)**

It is the highest chakra and is found at the top of the head. Its color is violet. Violet makes one feel evolved, exalted, and spiritually awake to the level of connection to all that is around youths element is space.it is believed to give a sense of enlightened, divinity and spiritual connection as this is taking place one gains unity with their inner being as well as clarity and wisdom.it is associated with the eagle.

## Psychological, physical, and behavioral issues

The blockage of the crown chakra will cause an individual to experience feelings of ingratitude to all aspects of their lives. They don't appreciate the gift of being alive. There being healthy causes them to be always unhappy. As a result, they become disillusioned, bored, melancholic, and restless. The physical issues developed by the individual will be exhaustion, chronic headaches, and poor coordination, consequently becoming less productive, be they working or students. These individuals will develop a tendency to always want sleep due to their lack of inspiration and confusion about what to do since they can't place what they want at a personal level and act according to it. They will thus seem to have a disconnection with their spirituality, which may lead them to engage in destructive activities as they have no belief in a superior being. Moreover, apathy and cynicism will be experienced by these people.

## Healing crown chakra

Sahasrara is best realigned through constant exercises. That can easily be incorporated into the daily lives; thus, one can perform them without disruption of their daily routine.

## Healing stones

These stones can be shaped into gems that one can carry around in their pockets and bags and seek them when they feel as if there is a threat to block their crown chakra. They can be worn as bracelets and necklaces as well as held during the meditation and yoga exercises. These stones include;

- Clear quartz is used to boost spiritual attunement so that one can gain clarity on what they want out of this life as individuals.
- Sugilite pushes off negativity as it grounds your spirituality to promote love.
- Selenite is a lovely stone that enables one to move past their roadblock of stagnation and propel forward to achieve their purpose.

## Importance of Chakra Healing

1. Chakra healing helps in maintaining and improve balance in the chakras for optimum performance.
2. The healing helps an individual to feel more grounded and secure.
3. Healing helps one to improve their communication, thus can express their needs.
4. Open chakras will enable one to establish boundaries in relationships.

5. The realignment will lead one to develop a higher and more profound sense of connection.
6. When one gains clarity and is in touch with themselves, they can give as well as receive love

# Chapter 7: Meditation for Deep Sleep

*"Meditation is like a gym in which you develop the powerful mental muscles of calm and insight." -- Ajahn Brahm*

Lack of sleep is a common problem in modern-day society. It is called insomnia, defined by the quality of the sleep and the feeling you have after sleeping- but not the number of hours you sleep or how easily you fall asleep. Even if one sleeps for 8 hours a night, but still feel fatigued and drowsy during the day, he/she may be experiencing insomnia. Insomnia can affect one's health in many ways.

There are several causes of why people do not get sleep at night or suffer from insomnia, which differs from one person to another. Insomnia could be because of emotional issues such as anxiety, depression, and stress. However, there are other causes such as someone going through a traumatic experience, taking meditations that affect sleep, health problems that interfere with sleep, excessive caffeine intake, and improper sleep environment, among others.

Therefore, having known the causes and consequences of lack of sleep. One must keep good practices which results in having a good sleep at night. One best way to help have a deep sleep at night is by meditation, and for this reason, we are going to take a look at the meditation techniques for deep sleep.

## Mindfulness Meditation Technique for Deep Sleep

Millions of people do have a hard time to fall asleep at night. It leads to daytime sleepiness, which leaves one feeling lousy, saps productivity, and may even harm his/her health. But there is a study which has shown that mindfulness meditation can help one to overcome this problem. This technique involves a mind-calming exercise that focuses on breathing and being aware of the present moment.

So, mindfulness meditation involves one focusing on his or her breath and then bringing the mind's attention to the present. It happens without one drifting into the concerns about the past, present, or even the future. It helps one to break away from everyday thoughts which evokes the relaxation response. However, this is not an exercise which makes one to go to sleep, but rather helps one to understand and increase awareness of his/her mind at night which results in sleep. One practice the mindfulness technique, ideally for about 20 minutes during the day. Below are the steps through mindfulness technique:

**Step 1**

The moment you are lying in bed, take deep breaths, breathing in through the nose and out through the mouth. Choose something to focus on, like a calming focus. It could be sound like a short prayer or a positive word like "peace" or a phrase such as "I am relaxed." When you choose the sound, say it repeatedly loudly or silently as you breathe in and out.

**Step 2**

Let go, and then relax. Do not worry about anything at all, but in case you notice that your mind wandered, all you have to do is take a deep breath and gently return to your attention and then to your chosen focus.

## Abdominal Breathing for Deep Sleep

During the day and at night in bed, breathing from the abdomen and shifting your attention to your breaths can help one relax. Some people like to lie down in a dimly lit room, listening to soft music, or closing their eyes as they focus on their breaths.

As you lie in your bed, try to place your hands on the belly. Breathe in and out, moving your hands gently over the belly. Putting your focus into this movement gets your mind off the busy thoughts and onto the body. It is a very calming exercise and can help you to get a good sleep. Practice this exercise when you lie down to fall asleep at night, also when you wake up at night and have trouble falling back to sleep. It is particularly so much help when you have your mind preoccupied or racing, something which is common among people who have insomnia.

Get a position in your bed that you are comfortable in, and let yourself relax begin to take note of your body and any other sensations you might be feeling. Try to feel the connection of your body and the surface you are sleeping on, relax your tension, and perhaps soften your muscles. Put all your attention on your body, but if your thoughts start to wander, something which is common when someone is in bed, try to redirect it back to your body. It takes time and a lot of practice to learn to focus your attention on your body only.

Start to notice the breath and the part where you feel it in your body, probably your abdomen, and then focus the attention on the full breath. Again, if your mind starts to wander, try to bring it back to your breath. Take a deep breath into your lower abdomen and feel it expand with air. Hold it for a few seconds, and then you release. Notice your belly falling and rising, and the air coming in and out for a few times. Imagine this air filling up the abdomen, and then going through the airways, over and over again. Do this repeatedly as you take note of the areas of your body where you feel tension, relax the tension by directing the breath into that area.

# Affirmation Meditation for Deep Sleep

This meditation is somehow similar to mindfulness meditation, as it requires one-pointed attention. But here, in place of focusing on the breath, you are replacing the distractions, which are making you stay awake with a positive affirmation such as "my mind is calm" or "I am at peace," etc. Only choose an affirmation that has significance for you. You could also use a mantra from let's say a particular faith tradition, instead of an affirmation. Psychologists have a belief that the thoughts which go through our minds as we try to fall asleep get deeply anchored in the subconscious. Therefore, positive affirmations do not only help you to fall asleep but also may have an uplifting residual effect.

Your body and mind need and deserves the rest, and using these positive bedtime affirmations can get you into a calm state of mind, so your body can get the rest it deserves. With every positive thought, it is like creating a space for what you want. Each time you repeat one of the positive bedtime affirmations of your choice, you invite peace in your mind and make a peaceful night sleep more of a reality.

Positive bedtime affirmations are the best tools for interrupting past or negative thought patterns. Therefore, one can use this to form new neural pathways in the brain, strengthening the beliefs which are helpful and beneficial to you while giving no or less attention to things which stresses you and keep you awake at night. By using this bedtime, positive affirmations are like talking out your body that it is okay to rest.

## Guided Meditation for Deep Sleep

Guided meditation is whereby you listen to the soothing voice of a meditation teacher in a meditation session to help you fall asleep. Meditation instructors give you a guide throughout the entire meditation session. An instructor may ask you to inhale deeply and exhale and relax your toes or legs. However, you should also note that this is not necessary you do with a guide by a specialist, but one can perform it alone.

Let's say you are using the help of the instructor. He/she may ask you to imagine a series of relaxing images. For example, some may invite you to imagine yourself at a beautiful sandy beach, and envision yourself happily seated along the water's edge as the wavelets tickle your feet.

The clouds, the mountains, and the oceans are the most commonly chosen scenes of imaginations. However, you can choose to focus on anything you want as long as it is calming. There are no rules about what one should imagine and focus on. Some people enjoy visualizing their office- brushing everything off his/her office desk and going to sleep. One only needs to pick a place he/she feels safe, and using imaginations, invite all the senses to explore it. It is simply because the brain doesn't often know the difference between what is real and what is not. For example, when you watch a horrifying movie, your adrenaline may go up, or when you start to salivate when you imagine yourself eating something.

Apart from helping with insomnia, meditation can help one to let go of negative thought patterns and emotions, giving one insight on how to deal with grief or trauma and thus encouraging healing. Therefore, meditation has a wide array of other benefits when diligently practiced. Meditation can also help to develop compassion towards other people. Yeah, a pretty nice and wholesome way to get to sleep! Goodnight!

## Counting Down for Deep Sleep

As you lie down comfortably in bed, you can start by a gaze upward, as a little eye strain can help you feel relax. Breathe into your abdominal and hold it, and as you let the breath out, let everything relax. Do this a couple of times. After this, you can then start to imagine yourself walking down the flight stairs or walking down a gentle hill as you count down from let's say 20, every number signifying the movement to the lower step, as you exhale with each imaginary step you make.

A lot of things you can with this technique, for example, you can start by breathing into and out your belly. Then go to progressive relaxation, walk down the stairs as you count down the number from 20, and then you go to the imaginary peaceful place of your choice.

## Gratitude Meditation for Deep Sleep

Gratitude meditation is a kind of meditation, whereby instead of one focusing on the breath, it requires you to concentrate on the things you are grateful for. It is one of the easiest and effective ways to fall asleep, as one never lacks anything to be grateful for. The things you are grateful for could be something small as having a nice coffee, or something big like your partner or your job. All you need here is to challenge yourself to think of the things you are grateful for in life. I am sure such things are uncountable, now you can use them to gain some sleep if you are having trouble falling asleep at night.

Deprivation of sleep can have a devastating impact on one's health and general productivity. Therefore, it is essential to put a lot of considerations in the quality of our sleep. And since sleeping has been proven to contribute to the healing process of our body, it is high time we get some good night sleep. The good news, as discussed above, is that you don't have to take medications for you to have a night of quality sleep. All you have to do is to put into practice one of the above meditation techniques for deep sleep and enjoy yourself a pretty good sleep.

# Chapter 8: Yoga Sutras

*"Our own physical body possesses a wisdom which we who inhabit the body lack. We give it orders which make no sense" --Henry Miller*

Yoga sutras are two significant words with Yoga incredibly based on asana, while the sutras associated with how to be your true self and to feel appreciated every moment. Understanding the concept of yoga sutras is thus important since it is primarily based on mind refinement, concentration, and focus. The focus, in this case, is based on an end perspective, as quoted by Bruce Lee, "The successful warrior is the average man, with laser-like focus.". The focus thus promotes a distinct perception and the ability of an individual to know themselves.

The chapter will describe the concept of yoga sutras, the eight limbs of yoga, and conclude with the practice of Samadhi. Necessarily, in Yoga Sutras of Patanjali, there are one hundred and ninety-five short verses which were compiled 350 CE to promote guided meditations and ensure that the focus and concentration are regulated to prevent suffering. However, the information regarding Patanjali is not widespread, as only a few individuals understand him. Interestingly, scholars get confused on whether Patanjali was just a name created or whether he was a person. The chapter will clearly address such claims and assumptions regarding Patanjali as well.

## The Concept of Yoga Sutras of Patanjali

The concept of yoga sutras of Patanjali is one of the aspects which continuously raises a lot of concerns and misunderstanding both to modern society and in the past. It is thus your essential role to clearly understand this concept to ensure that such misunderstandings are resolved. There is continuous citing of yoga sutras as one of the philosophical tools in the physical yoga that is practiced in today's world. This is done with an implication that both the past and the present society are based on one understanding.

It is crucial to understand that in traditional society, philosophy was given a first-hand since it not only helped in the establishment of practical and essential understanding, but it also promotes personal growth. However, this does not necessarily mean that modern society lacks the same concept. This is why the yoga sutras is evidently valid in society today. The yoga sutras adequately work in the present world since every individual is oriented towards concentration and focus, which are achieved through the two words yoga and sutras.

There are various basics about Patanjali, which are relevant in understanding the concept of Yoga Sutras, regardless of the lack of essential information of Patanjali. The information of Patanjali is not clear since there is no specific timeline as most of the authors tend to estimate his timeline to some fifth century of the common era. Critically, Yoga Sutras was writing in a Buddhist Hybrid and not a classical one, which is an essential indicator that there were some influences of Buddhism. Patanjali thus can be argued to have some Buddhism basics, which assisted him in ensuring that the concentration and focus of individuals were oriented towards one direction.

### Interpretation of yoga sutras

Getting a clear understanding and interpretation of yoga sutras is important since it will substantially assist you in differentiating various complexities that most individuals face as they don't understand themselves. In layman's language, yoga sutras simply mean strings. The yoga sutras are thus one hundred and ninety-five aphorisms, which is correlated to a specific philosophy called yoga in the traditional world. However, the term yoga has consistently used in Sanskrit to mean various aspects, especially advocating that a union is an essential tool in promoting concentration.

The interpretation of yoga sutras of Patanjali can be identified with pure concentration or discipline. Yoga, the philosophical tool that interprets the relationship between the human world and the human spirit. The yoga also advocates what extent can such spirit be freed from suffering through introspection as well as discipline. However, yoga addresses little regarding the postural. Yoga is thus an important aspect not only to the human spirit but to what extent it correlates with otherworldly affairs.

After adequately addressing what yoga means, it is thus vital to separately address Sutras to make you understand the difference between the two, after which you relate them without any difficulty. In contrary to yoga, sutras tend to be abstruse and dense, and in most cases, correlated to explanatory commentary. The truth regarding sutras is not only in the present word but also the traditional one since, in ancient times, both the commentaries were not only based on the explanatory aspect but also related to actions taking place within the community. In ancient times, it is also important to note that Patanjali clearly stated to the readers that his verses were not easy to understand, which is the opposite of what is taking place now.

Therefore, the two words yoga and sutras can be argued to be dualistic systems that are oriented towards differentiating matter (Prakriti) and spirit (Purusha). The aspect of salvation which the two terms advocated for can be argued to be one of the goals as it frees an individual from the cycle of death. In other words, the two systems ensure that the concentration and focus of an individual is monitored. The aspect of salvation is thus achieved through rational inquiry and deep meditation. It is, therefore, essential to ensure that you fully concentrate and avoid losing focus, which will substantially contribute to deep meditation.

In most cases and ancient contexts, yoga may be referred to as Samkhya and interpreted to ensure that every individual is driven towards achieving some of the critical requirements in today's society through the aspect of concentration, among others. It is thus essential to note that with clear interpretation and understanding of the concept of the yoga sutras of Patanjali, it, therefore, becomes easy to understand the eight limbs of Yoga, which will be addressed below. Yoga sutras are, consequently, an essential factor in understanding and taking part in deep meditation.

# The Eight Limbs of Yoga

The eight limbs of Yoga are necessarily the art of inner being and inner body. Yoga Sutras is thus an eightfold aspect that imparts spiritual aims and practices as well as intellectual wholeness among the individuals. Eight limbs, in this case, thus refers to the components which define Yoga sutras. The eight limbs are also vital since it is from them where deep concentration is necessarily based. The stipulated limbs include Samadhi (Absorption), Dhyana (meditation), Dharana (concentration), pratyahara (senses withdrawal), pranayama (breath control), asana (postures), niyama (observances) and Yama (abstinences). It is these eight limbs that makeup yoga sutras of Patanjali.

## 1. *Yama (Abstinences)*

Yama is the first limb of yoga sutras. It is associated with an individual's disciplined behaviors as well as integrity. It also relates to the golden rule, which states that do unto others or clean the house. Yama is essentially one of the social behaviors associated with how you treat the world around you as well as other people. They are basically moral principles which ensure that an individual is oriented towards achieving the most effective and reliable society.

Yama principles also guide an individual towards ensuring that they are not in conflict with others in society. The tenets of Yama include honesty and truth, which dictates that unless you are saying something, then you don't need to talk. The other principles include non-stealing, non-violence, non-lust, and non-possessiveness. These principles are what defines the Yama.

## 2. Niyama (Observances)

Niyama is the second limb of yoga sutras heavily dependent on Yama. Niyama essentially refers to observances. Niyama is dependent on the Yama since it also set the stage for doing the right things. In what Yama addresses as cleaning the house, it is essential to note that whenever the house is cleaned, then the stage is set for carrying out the right activities. Niyama is thus composed of spiritual observances and discipline regarding how you treat other individuals. It is, therefore, your essential role to ensure that you cultivate the inner being, which would necessarily lead to the right things. The observances are also known as the do's and are also divided into five categories, including purity, contentment, austerity, sacred text, and divine. The five categories determine your progress and relationship with others.

## 3. Asana (Postures)

The Asanas are also dependent on the Niyama since through the Niyama, a good stage is set for the Asanas. Asanas can be identified as the postures which are oriented towards disciplining the body. The aspect of discipline is geared towards achieving the aspect of concentration which yoga sutras of Patanjali advocates for. It is essential to understand that the prerequisite of meditation is concentration. These postures are thus important since they enable you to take care of your sense of unity, faith, and emotions to achieve deep meditation. Through yoga practice, your body is reattached, and thus your responsibilities and wisdom are adequately set. Regardless of being misquoted in today's context as health factors, Patanjali incredibly states that the primary role of the postures is for deep concentration.

### 4. Pranayama (Breath-control)

Just as the stage for Asana is set by Niyama, Pranayama is also dependent on Asanas as the same stage is set. Pranayama essentially rides the breath and thus is identified as a respiratory determiner. It is essential to understand that the emotions, the mind, and the breath are substantially correlated to each other, and thus, whenever one is affected, the other ones are also interfered with. Therefore, the measurement, retention, and control of breath are dependent on the pranayama, an indicator that it affects what is in mind, which eventually influences concentration and meditation. It is thus evident that concentration being a prerequisite of meditation; it is heavily dependent on the pranayama.

### 5. Pratyahara (Senses withdrawal)

Through Pranayama, a stage is adequately set for Pratyahara. Pratyahara ensures that there is a self-inward drawing of the sensory transcendence. It is a way of escaping the effects that are caused by stimuli. It thus enables you to stay aware of any sense without necessarily having any attention or attachment. In other

110

words, through pratyahara, it becomes easy to realize your senses without any stimuli, which in the real sense, may be detrimental. Pratyahara mostly takes place whenever you meditate since the mediation object absorbs your progress. It can thus be identified as the distractor of the senses. Whenever the senses are distracted, meditation immediately begins. Importantly, it is essential to note that the first five limbs of yoga sutras work together and are argued to be concerned with individual spiritual life. The last three limbs also work together to ensure that the mind is reconditioned.

### 6. Dharana (concentration)

As observed in other cases, through pratyahara, a stage is set for Dharana, which refers to deep concentration. Whenever the body is relieved from other distractors, concentration is enhanced. Whenever such distraction is removed, it also becomes easy to meditate. You should thus ensure that you slow the brain from thinking by significantly ensuring that you direct your attention to a particular object. Dharana is vital since it not only relieves you from stress but also ensures that the relationship senses are adequately improved. To know that the mind is concentrating, no time passing is observed.

### 7. Dhyana (Meditation)

A stage is set for Dhyana by Dharana since it involves meditation contemplation. Dhyana is achieved through uninterrupted concentration, which enables an individual to refrain from any distractor. There is an essential difference between Dharana and Dhyana since in Dharana, there can be cases of losing focus, which is not the same case as Dhyana. Meditation is crucial since it helps you find solutions to problems that affect your daily life.

### 8. Samadhi (Absorption)

Samadhi is the last limb of yoga sutras and intensively dependent on Dhyana since it is Dhyana, which sets its stage. In Samadhi, there is the emergence between object and subject. In this limb, the mediator comes to a divine world whereby there is a connection with all living things. It is also in this limb where there is a piece of understanding, which assists you in resolving various problems. It is thus essential to note that the eight limbs of yoga sutras are crucial to deep meditation.

## The Practice of Samadhi

Generally, Yoga is a spiritual based practice, and thus, the final stage is the Samadhi. Samadhi is an essential state of consciousness in which the awareness of an individual is dissolved. Samadhi is composed of various stages that are oriented towards the divine connection. The highest step that other stages rely on is the state of enlightenment. Samadhi is important since every individual is a spiritual being and thus requires a vital state of spiritual connection.

Samadhi thus essentially fits in your life, and it is important since it directly influences the decisions that you make. Samadhi is not a permanent state; thus, focusing on it does not necessarily mean that it would influence your progress whatsoever. To take part in Samadhi, you simply need to recognize yourself as a spiritual being and note every individual is a spiritual being. It, therefore, means that every being including animals is divine and thus requires a divine connection. Samadhi thus regulates most of the connection which you have with others and plays a significant role in deep meditation.

# Chapter 9: A Relaxing Meditation Script That Will Help You Relieve Stress

*"Your goal is not to battle with the mind, but to witness the mind."–Swami Muktananda*

You can consider trying meditation anytime you are stressed; that is, anytime you are feeling anxious, worried, and tensed, this is because meditation swipes away the day's stress bringing you inner peace. If you spend a few minutes daily in meditation, it can help you reinstate your calm and inner peace. Any person can practice meditation because it is simple, not expensive, and does not require special equipment, you can as well practice meditation anywhere whether at work during a stressful meeting or at home when you are stressed about something.

While practicing meditation, you focus all your attention and remove all the thoughts crowding your mind causing stress; it results in improving your physical, emotional well-being and your health overall, and all these will not end if you stop practicing meditation. Meditation can help you through the day as you attend to your daily activities and manage signs of certain health conditions, especially those worsened by stress such as:

- Depression
- Chronic pains
- Anxiety
- Cancer
- Heart disease
- Tension headaches
- Sleep problems
- High blood pressure
- Asthma
- Irritable bowel condition

If you have the above-mentioned symptoms, you need to visit a health expert to advise you on what you need to do because, in some cases, medication can worsen the symptoms related to specific mental and physical health problems, but some people do not believe in meditation. However, meditation can be beneficial in other treatments. There are several benefits of meditation which help in reducing stress, and they include:

- Increasing self-awareness
- Reducing negative emotions
- Gaining a new perception of stressful circumstances
- Increasing patience and tolerance
- Concentrating on the present
- Growing imagination and creativity
- Building skills to manage your stress

You should also know that meditation has been practiced for a long time. Initially, it was considered to help deepen understanding of the divine and spiritual forces of life, and nowadays, it is used for relaxation of mind and reducing stress; thus, meditation is a type of mind and body corresponding medicine.

## Types of Meditation

Meditation, in other terms, is a state of being relaxed, there are various types of relaxation techniques that have the components of meditation, and they all have a common goal of achieving inner peace and calmness.

### 1. Yoga

This is when you perform a series of postures and controlled breathing exercises, promoting a more flexible body, inner peace, and a calm mind. This requires a lot of concentration during that moment because as you move, the poses need a lot of balance. Your account should focus on the busy schedule you are having.

## 2. Mindfulness meditation

This is all about being mindful and aware of living in the present moment; in other words, you expand your awareness. You need to focus on what you are doing at that moment and not getting lost in other thoughts like during meditation, and you need to focus on the flow of your breath and let your emotions and thoughts pass as you observe them.

## 3. Guided meditation

This is all about using your senses, such as the sense of smell, sounds, taste, textures, and sights as much as possible. You form mental images of places or situations you find relaxing in your mind, and a teacher may guide you.

## 4. Mantra meditation

In this type of meditation, you are required to repeat a calming word silently, thought, or phrase to prevent distracting your thoughts.

## 5. Mystical meditation

This is just the same as mantra meditation though you are required to repeat the word, sound, or phrase in a specific way.

It allows your body to rest in a state of relaxation and your mind to achieve inner peace and calmness without concentration or using much effort. Mystical meditation is a natural and straightforward technique.

## 6. Qi gong

This technique includes meditation, physical movement, relaxation, and breathing exercises that aid in the restoration and maintenance of balance. Qi gong is part of Chinese traditional medicine.

## 7. Tai chi

This is where you perform a self-paced series of postures or movements slowly and gracefully while practicing deep breathing. Tai chi is a form of gentle Chinese martial arts.

# Various Tips to Use Relaxation and Guided Imagery Scripts in Relaxation

1. Begin with a short script, and when you practice, work up to longer texts. You should be able to add or delete contents where possible, and this is to modify the script for your preferences.

2. Record as you are reading the script slowly in a calm voice. A person's voice can be the best for inducing relaxation answers, and this is due to many people often answering best to the suggestions that they give to themselves. It is

easy for you to relax while listening to your voice, unlike listening to someone's voice.

3. Most of the time, you should pause. It is a common thing to read in a hurry, and what will look like a slow pace when reading sounds very slow when listening. In every phrase, you should take in two or three breaths. When you decide to pause in the middle of a sentence, it can be vital too.

4. Be attentive on saying every word clearly and with no hurry. It should not be that slow that it can distract. When you practice more, then it will assist in adjusting your reading skills.

5. You can playback the spoken script if you feel like it. Decide to use a piece of music that has no lyrics and will comfortably relax your mind.

6. You should be listening to the script with a low volume, and it should be an adjusted one that you won't strain yourself to hear. It should also be quiet enough that it can calm and relax.

7. More often, you should be able to listen to the relaxation audio and try to practice to learn how to relax.

Stress is a thing that is always around, and you can try at least two or three stress busters that you will possibly like. There are many relaxation scripts, as shown below.

**Visualization Scripts**

This is a method that you relax by picturing a relaxing scene, residence, or copy. You can have a try to visualization scripts like beach visualization relaxation, color relaxation, forest visualization relaxation, amongst many more.

## Steered Imagery Scripts

Theses scripts will provide you to relax and have positive changes. It can also be used to visualize positive activities, deviations, or accomplishments.

## Easing for Nervousness Respite

This kind will precisely target at reducing anxiety at the moment by comforting the mind and the body. In this case, it will include reduction scripts for dealing with panic occurrences, discharging apprehension, and managing with unease, fright, and tension.

## Directed Meditation Scripts

You will be able to relax when you focus. Use decide to use your guided meditations to help in calming your mind and relaxing your body to accomplish health, curing, or the capability to comfortably rest. The guided meditation scripts have an inclusion of self-esteem relaxation, breathing meditation, pain relief relaxation, anchoring relaxation, among many others.

Anxiety relief scripts are explicitly aimed at reducing anxiety at the moment by calming down the brain and physique. The relaxation scripts, in general, have addressed a concern that you experience most of the time, extra with anxiety disorders, fears, panic attacks, or conditions that will bring stress. You can teach yourself to reduce stress, manage its symptoms that come along, and match up with panic attacks. A lot of anxiety scripts will put their focus on particular situations like when you have the anxiety to speak to the public, and other writings will aim at the signals or signs of distress. You should learn how to manage or organize your anxiety signs at the moment and slowly create the skills for long term anxiety relief by most of the time doing more rehearsals on the relaxation methods.

Such scripts will help you to gain perspective and manage daily strains. You can imagine taking a walk along the white beach. This is where you will be able to hear the gulls and gentle rolls of the sea waves. When your feet sink in the warm white sand, you will feel relaxed and safe. This is a place that you have been looking for, and you will contact as you own the beach, and it is yours alone.

In this busy and distracted world of ours, the concept of being mindful and to practice guided imagery are invaluable gifts that you can offer to your kids or family. When they are growing and getting to face new challenges, guided imagery will give the kids a lifelong tool that can assist in impacting their confidence, deal with depression, and be able to access inner knowledge. A lot of kids nowadays are facing sensory overload. Despite technology being a leisure activity, it has stimulated your senses and reduced personal contacts and reduces the amount of exercise that you put yourself into, like relaxing.

# Chapter 10: The Easiest Meditation Techniques to Increase Will Power

*"What is now proved was once only imagined."* — **William Blake**

Our will power is continuously put through its paces, making it harder to control ourselves in an increasingly chaotic world. Luckily, we are not born with fixed willpower; like anything else, willpower can be cultivated and increased. After all, studies have shown that willpower breeds success. Training the brain with meditation helps fortify your strength (self-control) in dealing with the physical circumstances.

When you practice meditation once a day, every day makes it easier to control your focus, energy, and tenacity when trying new things that require dedication and effort. Guided meditations are designed to help boost our willpower to reduce the negativity in our lives, like stress and bad habits, and focus on love, positive energy, and behaviors. Meditation not only increases willpower, but it also reduces stress and increases our ability to learn.

## Concentration Meditation

This practice takes about 15 minutes, and it focuses on concentrating your mind on one thing. On different days, the focus of your mind will be different. You can choose to do the exercise in five, ten, or fifteen minutes.

Sit still with your eyes closed for the proposed length of time and resist the urge to indulge your impulses. When you think you are still is when your body itches- try not to scratch. Do not move, allow the noise and the world around you to continue their flow but do not engage. When time lapses, finish the meditation and acknowledge the stillness you managed to achieve. With time, your mind will learn to remain still and focus on one thing at a time.

## Breathing Meditation

This exercise focuses on the feeling of breathing. Close your eyes and inhale. Note "inhale" in your mind, and "exhale" when you breathe out. When your mind wanders off, allow it to label all the other sensations of the body, such as "back itchy," or "sound of dogs barking," etc. You can also ask yourself how it feels to breathe. Is your body relaxing? Can you feel the tension leaving your body? Then pull your mind back to breathing. Allow this rhythmic movement of the mind and thoughts from the breathing pattern, to the sensations.

Breathing meditation will help you become more aware of your environment and assist with impulse control in response to your surroundings. It also activates the brain's prefrontal cortex, quieting the stress and cravings.

## Guided Relaxation

Guided relaxation uses several techniques that may be used separately or in combination with each other. It may last as long as ten minutes and helps reduce impulses that trigger automatic behaviors. Guided relaxation uses abdominal breathing, visualization, progressive muscle relaxation, and mindfulness.

You will learn to breathe deeply as you imagine a serene environment using guided imagery. This sort of visualization activates the imaginative and sensory faculties of your brain. Relaxation meditation may also focus on relaxing the muscles so that you may feel the difference between tense and relaxed muscles when you are responding to stimuli. Mindfulness techniques are relaxing because the mind does not cling on one particular thought. It wanders and hops from thought, emotion, sensation, etc. Mindfulness meditation is about being present in the now.

## Desensitization Using Meditation

This practice is used to control fear, anxiety, stress, anger, and other forms of psychological trauma. It is useful as a healing/

coping tool. This meditation exercise begins with relaxing your body, use relaxation meditation techniques to bring your body and mind to calm. Then, invite your mind into an environment that causes anxiety for you. The situation may cause you anger, distress, uneasy, etc. If the emotions become overwhelming, and it starts to feel less like meditation and more of trauma, return your mind to the feeling of relaxation.

This technique does not always work, especially for fragile people. If you are beginning to heal, it is best to start with other forms of meditation before you try out this practice. However, the exercise helps you handle stressful situations better with what is called "graduated exposure."

## Compassion Meditation

Self-compassion is of tremendous importance when making a difficult life change in your life, such as healing from trauma. Self-love will help you overcome challenges that may seem impossible. It involves the repetition of specific phrases that shift the attention from judgment, dislike, and ridicule, to caring, love, and understanding.

In this meditation practice, the instructor will ask you to come up with thoughts and memories when you felt love for yourself, care, happiness, and contentment. You will also be asked to imagine sending thoughts of love, peace, and affection to the people dearest to you. Assume that with every breath you inhale love from them, and exhale love and affection back to them.

## Yoga Nidra

This practice takes approximately 30-minutes. It promotes body relaxation while maintaining alertness of the mind. Yoga Nidra is also referred to as dynamic sleep, where the balance between wakefulness and sleep is nurtured.

This form of guided meditation will take you through the active thinking stage, then the relaxing, thoughtless, second stage, the instructor takes you deeper into a third, slowed state of thought. In this state, thinking has been considerably slowed, and it is possible to learn copious amounts of information at this stage (super-learning). Finally, the body and mind enter the last phase, known as the delta stage, where restorative functions happen. Your organs regenerate and heal, and the body releases all the pent-up stress. Do not try to skip the steps as every phase has its purpose, and the therapeutic process will not be reached if parts of the exercise are omitted.

You can practice these techniques one at a time, and do not feel pressured to master them all. If one does not work for you, it is okay, move on to the other. Meditation is not a quick-fix solution; therefore, dedicated practice is necessary for the desired outcome.

The next time you feel downcast or undisciplined, retreat to your meditation and remember that willpower is a muscle, and you have it within yourself. Resisting the power of your thoughts is difficult, but once mastered, you can as quickly learn to overcome other habits and temptations. The more control you gain over your internal turmoil, the better placed you will be to deal with your immediate surroundings. Constant practice will yield gradual improvement as meditation is the most straightforward and effective way to improve willpower.

# Conclusion

Thank you for making it through to the end of *Guided Meditations for Self-Healing: Beginners Meditation to Heal Your Body. Mindfulness Meditation Including Breathing, Vipassana Script, Chakra Healing, Yoga Sutras, Meditation for Deep Sleep, And More.* Let us hope that it offered you valuable information that you need to achieve your goal of overcoming worry. Simply because you have finished reading this interesting book does not mean that nothing is left to learn about how to improve your wellness and happiness; expanding your horizons is the only way to find the mastery you seek.

Your next step should be to take action on whatever you have learned to ensure that yourself and everyone you care about do not live in fear and worry. In case you feel that you still need help in getting started to address all the worries in your life, you need to develop an action plan that will enable you to implement most of the proposed meditation tips to happiness and increased energy.

Studies have shown that stress can affect the greatest part of our lives. It does not only cause physical and health effects but also creates more fear towards leading a happy and peaceful life. By setting up life goals and objectives and addressing the thoughts that influence our wellbeing through meditation, you can easily get rid of life stressors. Go ahead and set your own goals and plan of action, and once you have completed all the recommended meditation strategies, you will be happy that you made a move.

Finally, if you found this book useful in any way, a review on Amazon is always appreciated!

Made in the USA
Las Vegas, NV
07 December 2020

12282085R00075